GRAFFITI VERITE' 18 (GV18)
Special 1974 Commemorative Reissue Series

IMPRESSIONS

Magazine of the Arts

Volume 1 Number 3
Original Publication: October 1975

Reissue for Educational & Historical Reference Use Only

Disclaimer:
All Promotional Advertisements, Store Addresses, Events, Telephone Numbers, Magazine Location, Product Sale Prices and Magazine Subscription information within the Original Publication issue are no longer, in most cases, in existence and/or applicable.

Please direct all inquires regarding the Special 1974 Commemorative Reissue of the GV18 IMPRESSIONS MAGAZINE (2012) to :

IMPRESSIONS MAGAZINE

c/o BRYAN WORLD PRODUCTIONS
P.O. Box 74033 Los Angeles, CA 90004 USA
website: www.graffitiverite.com
e-mail: bryworld@aol.com

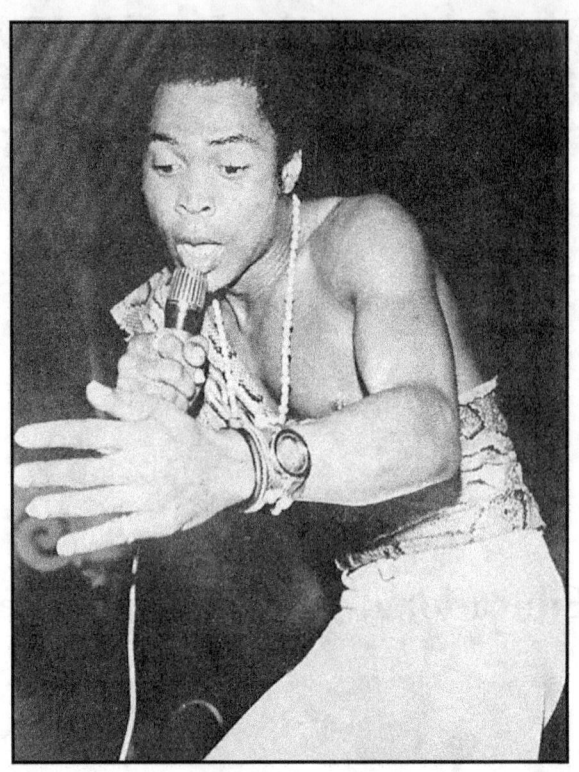
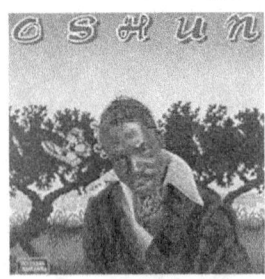 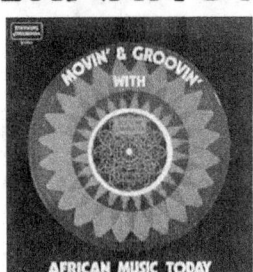 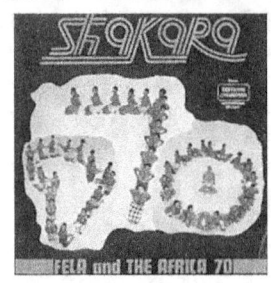 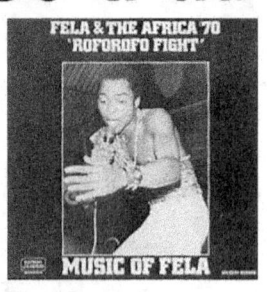 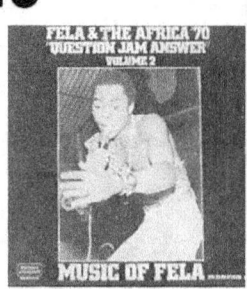

IMPRESSIONS

VOL. 1 NO. 3

MAGAZINE OF THE ARTS

contents

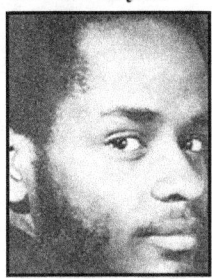

Publisher
Robert Bryan

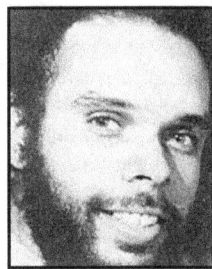

Editorial Director
Calvin Wilson

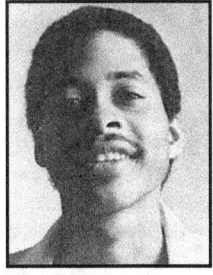

Art Director
Herb Henry

Special Assignments Editor
Hector Lino, Jr.

Contributing Editors:
Brenda Bailey
Nikki Coleman
Bob Wisdom
Michael Hyatt
Yvonne Moran

Music:

34   Bob Marley   'You've got to love yourself before you can   by Bob Bryan
      love Reggae.' (Interview)

4   Novella!   Novella Nelson, singer, actress and director
      talks with Bob Bryan.

28   Eternal Rhythms of Earl 'Fatha' Hines   by Nikki Coleman

52   The Roots of a Jazz Singer - Joe Lee Wilson   by Brenda Bailey

58   Jazz Notes: The Revolutionary Growth of An Ensemble   by Bob Wisdom

Theater:

40   Ed Bullins   by Calvin Wilson

38   The Confrontation   by Martie Charles

Art:

36   Viola Burley

8   Colleen Cannon

26   Mel Wright (photographs)

32   Bob Bryan (photo essay)

18   Ed Leak (photo essay)

50   Bob Ellison (photo essay)

Film:

17   On Film   by Hector Lino, Jr.

13   D'urville Martin: Facing the Challenges of the Evolving
      Film World.

54   Ron Van Clief - The Black Dragon   by Bob Bryan

Literature:

46   Reflections of John Oliver Killens - Novelist, Essayist,   by Bob Bryan
      Playwright.

9   Conversation with a Native Son - James Baldwin   by Maya Angelou

Feature:

20   God's Touch - Chapter from *Coltrane: A Biography*   by C. O. Simpkins, M.D.

Nutritional Well-Being:

25   Fasting and Your Spiritual Health   by Brenda Bailey

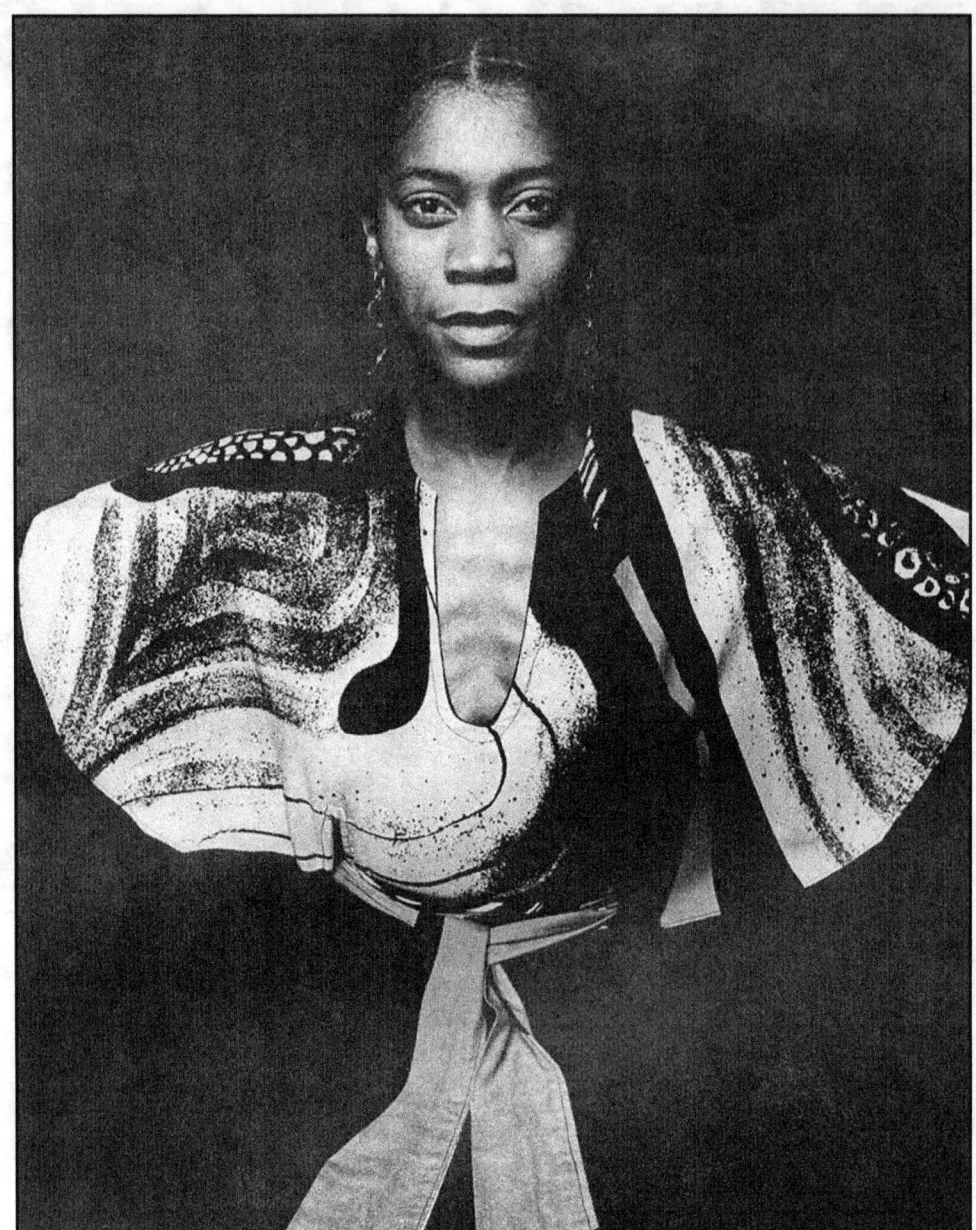

novella!

novella nelson, singer, actress and director talks with bob bryan

Impressions: Novella, you're a multi-talented lady whose talents have been expressed in directing, acting and singing. At what point did you realize that the arts would be a serious part of your life?

Novella: Well, I don't know. I can't answer that and say 1963 or 1967. My mother and father tell me that they have always known that I would go into the arts. I was a science major, getting a degree in bio-chemistry. But one day I walked out of school and said, well, I'm going to try it, and they were not surprised. They resented it, got up-

tight. "My daughter is in the theater," and all that kind of stuff. But once I was in the profession they accepted it. I'm at the point of it being the thing that I respond to the most. I consider myself someone who is creative, and to create is to just constantly do, and the way I create is in the arts. But I don't know the point when...

Imp: While you were a bio-major were you involved in the arts?

Novella: Oh, yeah. One day — I've said this so many times — I took a speech class, which was an acting class. It was the first

time that I'd ever worked on stage and I kind of liked it. So I was stimulated, but it didn't take me away from the science thing. Then I got more involved, in college. In high school I was not involved in drama.

Imp: What college did you go to?

Novella: Brooklyn College. I'm Brooklyn-bred.

Imp: Reflecting on your life, can you trace the major events in your life that helped to shape where you are today?

Novella: I'm just discovering them now. I really am. I'm one of those people who don't remember all of the things about my childhood. I got my mother alone the other week and I asked her lots of questions. Because I could not remember. But someone said to me, "You remember what you're supposed to remember. If you don't, it's because you're not, so don't even get hung up on it." So that's true, you know. There's just too many things, Bob. It's not this thing, this week, or that thing three years ago. There's just too many things that have placed me where I am now, there's just too many things.

Imp: Are there any particular ones that stick out in your mind?

Novella: There's been a couple, but I don't know if I want to talk about those. Times that have made me reaccess who I am and recognize that I have to look inside. There was a child once. A little Rastafarian child in Jamaica who really introduced me to the Rasta community. Her name was Christine. She was in many ways older and wiser than I. She was only 8 or 9, and she taught me how to walk on the water. I had gone to stay with some friends in Kingston and then I went out to the beach, met her, and then lived with the Rasta community. They live near the water. That became a very meditative time for me, a very quiet time. And it was because of her that they really welcomed me. I don't know if I'll ever see her again.

Imp: Have you been with the Rastafarians ever since?

Novella: No, I'm not a Rastafarian, but then I'm not in any order now. They don't push you to join, which makes them very pleasant to deal with. During the weeks that I spent with them, I went into mineral water so I could clean myself out.

Imp: Did you bathe in the mineral water?

Novella: Yes. It was a little place that they showed me. You know, like if you live in a small town, the nooks and crannies...they shared it with me. But it was really because of her. It was funny though. When it was time for me to go she knew that I would never see her again, but I was living in a fantasy saying that we would write each other and all that. But she knew that I was not going to be able to write. She really understood, because I didn't have an address and she didn't have one. So there was nowhere to write her or anything like that. So that's what I meant by her wisdom. And I was still dealing with another kind of fantasy. Such an experience I would never forget, one of many. But, Bob, I've been lucky like that. I've met a few people whose energies have opened me and who have taught me much.

Imp: When you think of yourself as a little girl, what are the recurring thoughts?

Novella: I use the word "shy." Most people don't think that I'm shy. So maybe it's the wrong word. But I was a quiet child, and maybe the word is not "shy." The one thing I did get from my mother, talking to her the other day, is that I accessed people before I communicated with them. I remember that I used to read a lot when I was a child. I had, and still have, very few friends. I do not use the word loosely. I know lots and lots of people and have a great love for most people, but I have very few friends. Very few, very, very few.

Imp: Do you think that it's because of your meditative nature, or is it that you just don't relate to masses of people?

Novella: I don't know. Someone said that that's a Sagittarian trait, that we talk a lot, that it looks as if you're getting to know who we really are. But we have saved that secret closet, so that we are really only telling you a part of who we are.

Imp: Who were some of the people that you identified with when you were growing up?

Novella: Well, I never thought of things in those terms. There were a number of people. I liked my grandfather. Once, when I was out of school and I had first moved down to the Village, I found that New York University was giving a psychiatric program, free. So I said, 'Wow, maybe I should go into analysis.' It only lasted about three weeks — so don't get hung up into it on any level. So I applied. They asked me why I thought I needed psychiatric help and I said if I knew I wouldn't be coming to you. That was the only sentence, and they called me into a meeting immediately. They gave lots of exams, and the purpose of one of the exams was to determine who in history you would like to be like. So that's the same kind of question, you know. So I said, well, the person I responded to the most was my grandfather. Because when he smiled, he genuinely meant it, and he had a great love for the human race. He was a Human Being. Well, they said "No, no, no...we mean like Cleopatra and people like that." (Laugh). I said, "No good." So I guess it would be my grandfather that I respond to. But I don't think that I would ever want to be completely like him. But he was very special to me. And I loved my grandmother! They were a nice couple. She was quite proper and he was very basic. They tell me that I speak like my grandmother, so I must have gotten this voice, the way I...My hands, I was singing one time and some friends came down and they said, your grandfather will always live with you because your hands are just like his.   And I had not thought of that, that he used his hands a lot. They tell me that I speak a lot like my grandmother because she was clever with words and he was very basic.

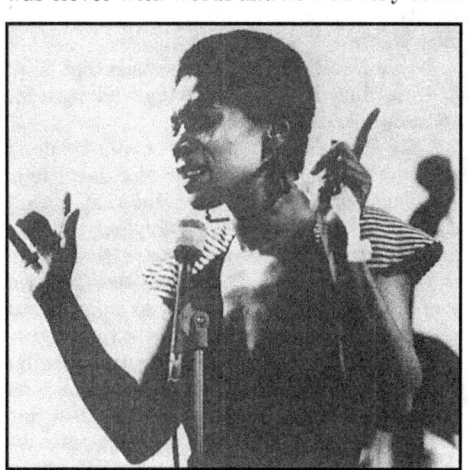

Photo by Bob Ellison

He was straight and what have you and she would be, "Nathaniel," she called him that (laughs). So I think I have elements of both of them in me. But I'm just like my mother! The more I grow, the more I see it in me. Just like her...

Imp: When you approach a new song, what do you look for before you include it in your repertoire?

Novella: Wow. That's really weird. Some days it just depends on how I feel. I can hear a tune and go "Wow!" Some tunes I have to live with for months and months and months. If someone sends me a song, I listen to it, but it really does depend on my mood. If I'm feeling sad, happy tunes may not help me on that day. But for a sad tune I may go, "Oh." Now, I may be happy the next day but whatever the emotion was, you know. I really get tunes from emotions, from how I feel. Now, I may not do them for a long time, but then some songs I sing all the time in cabs and eventually I just add them to my repertoire. I sing them walking down the steeet...keeping singing them.

Imp: Were there any acting roles that you've really enjoyed compared to others that you've played?

Novella: I don't know if I enjoyed it, but it is just leaving me, it is really just leaving me. My spirit is getting longer. Because it was without a doubt, I think, the role that I was the freest with, the concentration I was the best with, the commitment to the character was the strongest with, and I was very young when I did that. I did that in college and I was about 19 or 20 then. But when you're younger you're like a child, freer and less inhibited, less protective with yourself on those levels. I could be her in a second (she character). I mean, I could just turn her on and off and just move to her emotions. And it's only in the last year or two that she's leaving me; if that makes sense to you. I mean, I have always felt old and I am feeling younger each day! She is going away! Thank you Jesus!!! (Laughs)

Imp: Many black actresses are forced to do roles that are very stereotyped. It is very rare indeed when you see any individual kind of black woman that comes through real. What kind of black women would you like to see written about, that you would like to play the role of?

Novella: Wow, that's hard; we are not alike. There are lots of lives...

Imp: Well, as a personal thing, how do you feel?

Novella :(Comically) I don't want to play no singers (laughs)

Imp: You mean you don't want to be Diana Ross? (Laughs)

Novella: I don't want to be anything, you know. I ain't negating Diana Ross, because she is out there with a black man that has put her through. Whatever else people deal with, you've got to deal with Diana Ross and Berry Gordy. You've got to deal with that! It is a positive thing you have to look for. A black man believed in her and said, "Hey." He believed in her and put her through. I mean, he *believed* in her and he has come through along with her, too. So don't misunderstand that. And he wasn't in a position at first, but whatever his ego thing was, his security must have been enough so that she could be out there in front on some level. I don't even know their relationship. I don't want to even get into it. All I can respond to is a classic example of two people working together, male and female, and its coming forth. I just don't want to play no singers, that's all.

Imp: Well, what are some of the realities for a black actress-singer that you think that other black women should take into consideration when they're thinking about going into theatre?

Novella: Remember that it's a business.

Imp: Above all?

Novella: I think so. Don't lose the reality that it's a business. Because it'll just make it easier, you know.

Imp: How does that help you to approach it?

Novella: Well, I treat my creativity as something very special. I have been rejected a lot. I mean, people may not get to that, but I was fired from the first play I was in, and I've been told that I can't have a job. I've had people play around with me in terms of yes, we're going to do something, or, no, we're not. So I had to get very secure in my own belief, in my own artistry, and that's the first thing that you cannot trust, the words of the people. That doesn't mean that you can't enjoy that they respond to you, but you have to believe in your own creativity. You really have to believe that you have it. Now that doesn't mean that you don't or cannot learn, be fed and be nourished. But you have to believe that you are creative. That's first. Then when you get out there in this profession, you have to understand that, for whatever the reasons. You may be too short, you may be too tall, or somebody's going to use their friend. Sometimes you are rejected for that, and that's cool.

Imp: ...and it has absolutely nothing to do with...

Novella: With who you are or your creativity, and also, some people just don't see your creativity. On that day, they just don't see it. That's one thing that you have to deal with. And I think that you have to get off ego trips, which is the most difficult thing, but we have to — the black artist especially. We really do have to get off egos in the traditional form, and I know that is very hard because you are selling yourself in your performance. It's not like you can look at the painting or the book and say, well, it is completed. So that you can see it, you can't see yourself. You, personally, are rejected, but you have to be willing to take work. I'm not asking people to do things that are alien to them, that cause them internal tension. But some actors may reject roles that I think they have no reason to reject. Because we know that you're an actor and that you need a job and the only way that you can perfect your craft is if you work.

Imp: Yet so many people attack black actors who play particular roles, saying that they provide bad images of ourselves. "Why did you take that role, it's so negative, etc."

Novella: Ahhh, that's that elite group that I keep telling you about. (Laughs) That is that elite group who I just question. I mean, I can't live my life by that isolated group who are no longer attached to any of those communities. I'm not saying to go against your own internal beliefs, because it ain't about hassling yourself. But if you see a role that you really want to do, then the problem is if you're not going to do it, somebody else is going to do it.

Imp: Do you feel that actors/actresses have a social responsibility? Let's say a role like Priest in *Superfly*, it had a profound effect on...

Novella: I loved *Superfly*. If they really get to it, all the Black people went to see *Superfly*. So whoever was talking, they were not talking for the community. Because those people who did that film, if they had looked at the community...and I'm not saying that there weren't things in it. But I enjoyed it.

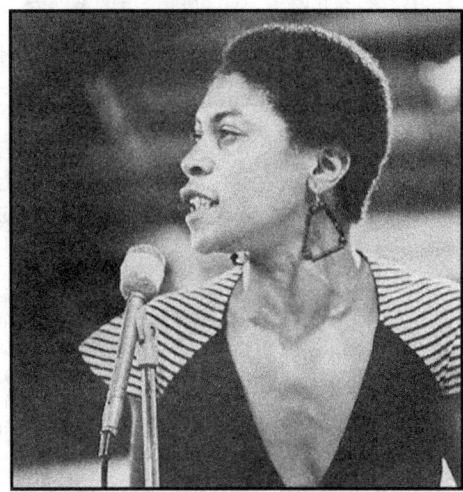

Photo by Mel Wright

Imp: On what level?

Novella: As a movie! A Hollywood romantic movie. It was entertaining. I liked *Lady Sings the Blues* too. I thought it was a fabulous movie. They're unreal, you know, if people get to this reality. For me they're unreal. There are some movies that come out that are supposed to be life, but they're replicas of life. 'Cause you know that *Superfly* was not real. He got away (laughs).

Imp: It seemed as if a lot of people, for whatever reasons, actually copied his lifestyle.

Novella: Oh, they just dressed like him.

Imp: In some cases they even adopted his attitude towards life.

Novella: I don't know, I really don't know. All I know is that for a while everybody looked like *Superfly*. But that wasn't going to last forever. Everybody, for a while, had an Afro. They don't all have them anymore. Anyway, it's only those few isolated people who want to see, so I do believe that everything is political in a way. I mean, how you dress, how you present yourself, what you eat is political. But there are fads that come and go, and don't misunderstand me, but I don't think anything's wrong with us having all kinds of movies. I really don't. The problem with *Superfly* might be that it was

the only one. So that there was no other alternative. I loved *Superfly*. I really did. It is never about negating anybody. If you can learn something from something, then it is positive. If you can't, then maybe you've got to let it go. I don't know what to say.

Imp: It often happens that some of our most gifted performers are not given the proper acclaim that they should. Do you feel that's because of non-access to media or the audience not being attuned to the artist's brilliance, or do you think that it's a combination of the two?

Novella: Oh, I think that it's got to be both. There are artists that you have not heard of, just because you're not in the theatre. For example, there are actors that you've never heard about. There are some singers that I could name for you. There is a sister by the name of Bernice Regan that I heard in 1968 in Atlanta. She's now with the D.C. Repertory. I don't know if she'll ever come to N.Y. I have not heard her sing since then, but that is a moment that will live with me forever! I mean that Sister can sing! I mean, I don't even know her. We've never met or communicated, but I remember that. She could sing. That's just one example. There are dancers that I've seen, you know. Ones who do not have media exposure as much as we'd like. We are not in a position to continually produce. We are not producing. We do not have the economic arm, and also we don't support each other. Whether we admit it or not, we want Broadway shows, to go to Broadway. We are still striving in the same way; we are not planning alternatives, necessarily.

Imp: How do you feel that we can rectify that?

Novella: I don't know. If I had some of those answers to those questions I would be doing them because it ain't about talking about 'em. It's just about doing 'em. And there are people who are. For example, Ellis Haizlip is the only producer of a Black television show. His media thing has been Black. Woody King has only related to black writers, and there are those personalities who I think, with whatever they do, in whatever field that they're in, be it T.V., be it theater, as Woody has been in the theater, the thing that I have to respond to in some personalities are that they are intent and bent on thrusting forward other minorities. So you have to deal with that.

Imp: We have a limited amount of Black publications, yet they don't place enough emphasis on or give space to Black Theater and...

Novella: Then we question what it is...but they sell well, don't they? They do, but they only relate to the people who are more established. They stay with established personalities.

Imp: What innovation in the theater would you like to see come about?

Novella: I'd like to see Edgar White on Broadway, Charles Fuller, Clay Gloss and lots of other writers that I can think that nobody's every heard of. We are going to have to work together, we really are going to have to do lots together, we really are going to have to do lots of homework. Understanding that it's always competitive.

Imp: Do you believe that there's such a thing as the Black Aesthetic?

Novella: What does that mean? I don't know what it is! I have heard the term and I have heard it defined about seven different ways. If you want me to take the word *Black* as it is in in the dictionary and *Aesthetic* as it is in the dictionary and try to define it...I don't know what it is. I have trouble with the English language. I don't understand what these words mean. I really don't. I know what I like, but I don't understand it.

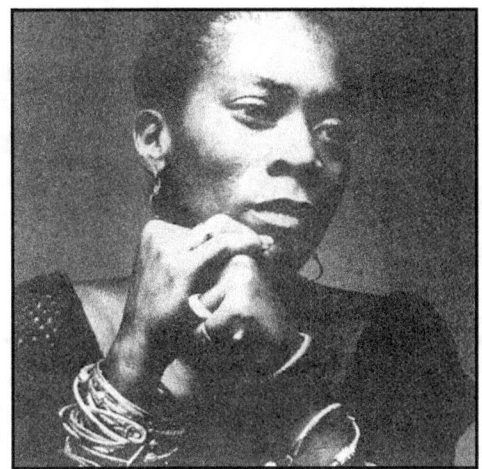

Photo by Toshi

Imp: Can an actress deal with a role that she can't identify with?

Novella: OK. This is something that I can say to all actresses. Everybody reads their roles. I don't read roles; I read the play. It is about reading the play. In terms of my technique, I am one link in a chain to make an entire objective to what the writer has written. Now, how do I serve the play and who is my character in terms of the rest of the play? That's all. There are some characters that I have difficulty with. Oh God, she's so negative, and stuff like that. But I have rejected very little as an actress, contrary to most people. I have done lots of repertory theater. I had not gotten hung up about working in N.Y.C. I'm not caught up into stuff like that. I have left two Broadway plays.

Imp: Because you got tired of if?

Novella: Well, I had made the money that I had wanted to make at that time. I should have saved a couple more dollars, but I was in *Purlie* for a very short period of time. I just don't reject work. I respond to work. I really don't deal with it as Broadway now. I really have, somehow, for my own health and my own sanity; I can't get caught up into 'Oh, I'm on Broadway', or 'Off Broadway', for my own sanity. It's because of the theatre, or I like the play and, "Hey," I might as well do that play.

Imp: What are the magic elements that make a fabulous actress?

Novella: That's very personal, I think. Concentration, commitment to the role. A certain charisma that you can't explain. Some talents just soar. I think that some actresses

will do some things better than others. But they are not the same kinds of personalities, so I don't want to narrow myself and say that I want to see just that. Because we're all textures and shapes and emotions. So I'm not going to zero myself in and say that I would like to see a woman who has this or that, etc....As for me, again, my intent is to serve the writer, not to get caught up into my own trip, but to serve him. There have been a number of plays where I could have gone off...I've never gone off in a play.

I have never let my ego shoot out and do special kinds of things. I don't even sing the same in a play, because it comes out of a character, and therefore it's different than the way I am off-stage. I'm not saying that there are parts of my personality that don't come through, but I really try to serve him. From a singing point of view, it is personal. It is trying to communicate, not necessarily my emotions, so that it will touch someone else. Because their experience may not be mine, but the emotion — we get angry; now, how do we let that anger out? So I'm coming from a personal experience. But you can feel anger if you understand what that is. I have great respect for audiences, because I believe that I am there to share with them, otherwise I could sing alone and I choose not to sing alone. I choose to share, but it is a personal emotional statement, coming out of me, that I'm trying to communicate.

Imp: Do you feel that at this time you have a range of material that expresses Novella?

Novella: Oh yeah. It's just begun, hopefully. When I first started singing, I think most of the songs were in search of this communication. I wanted to make it very clear to everyone that I was singing out of my experiences, that I am a black woman. I didn't trust me or them to just know it from just looking at me, so that most of the tunes that I selected just reemphasized that. I'm trusting me more, and in trusting me more, trusting the audience more, so that I can sing from many areas of myself as opposed to one or two. When I first began, I was just giving touches of specific areas of who I am, and I'm hopefully freeing myself, just me, Novella. So that I can now allow some of the other vulnerabilities of Novella to come through. That's what I'm striving for, so that I can sing, 'cause I don't think that I've been singing. I'm just beginning to sing, if that makes sense to you.

Imp: Who is Novella now?

Novella: I don't know. I just know that I've only shared part of my creativity and I don't know all of it myself. I'm just discovering things about myself, but I'm trusting me more, so that I can share it more. I have drawn from many artists and I know that I've absorbed from every artist that I have respect for. All of them that I have absorbed from, hopefully, have molded me into whoever I am evolving into.

Imp: Someone I spoke to this morning compared you to Nina Simone, and I asked how so, and she said in terms of strength.

Novella: Please, please (laugh). You hear me say that I'm trying to get vulnerable, not

strong. I think people misinterpret...I have lots of energy, so it's concentrated. People can call that strength if they want to. I don't deal with that word. I just have lots of energy and that energy is projected out. STRENGTH ... please!

Imp: Black theater has gone through a transformation from the 60's into the 70's. How do you interpret the shift of Black theater in terms of where it appears to be headed?

Novella: I don't think it's any different than the world. The 60's was the 60's, quote, "the revolution."

Imp: Has the revolution taken another form now?

Novella: Why are you asking me that question? Well, I don't see anybody on the streets with guns. People are trying to make money. So it's different. I think the theatre is the innovator but an expression of what is. People can tell me all they want that we create, but we take what is and show how it is, whether we like it or not. Now I don't know any writer, be he green, blue, black, white or red....When I was in English class years ago, they used to talk about how Ibsen had written *A Doll's House* or one of those plays. At that time it was "new." And I said, "That's crap, that wasn't new, it was just the first time somebody wrote about it." So I question whether or not we are innovators in anything that I feel people can identify with. I may have emotionally said it so that a vast majority could listen. Aretha sang *Doctor Feelgood*; it wasn't new but she sang it in a way that we could emotionally identify with. But it wasn't new, women have felt that way for years and years. So I question whether the artist has that weight and responsibility, and it doesn't mean that he shouldn't say what he feels and believes in, in terms of objectives. There are very few geniuses who just create. There are new forms, political forms; they are out there. It's just a matter of catching them.... If the artist is the innovator, I guess part of his responsibility, in terms of his innovation, is to explore himself more deeply. The more you get into yourself, the freer you are to let it out. ✿

Ed. note: The record album *novella nelson* is available in select record stores. For more information write to:

Allevon
160 W. 95th Street
New York, New York 10025

Cover photograph by Bob Bryan

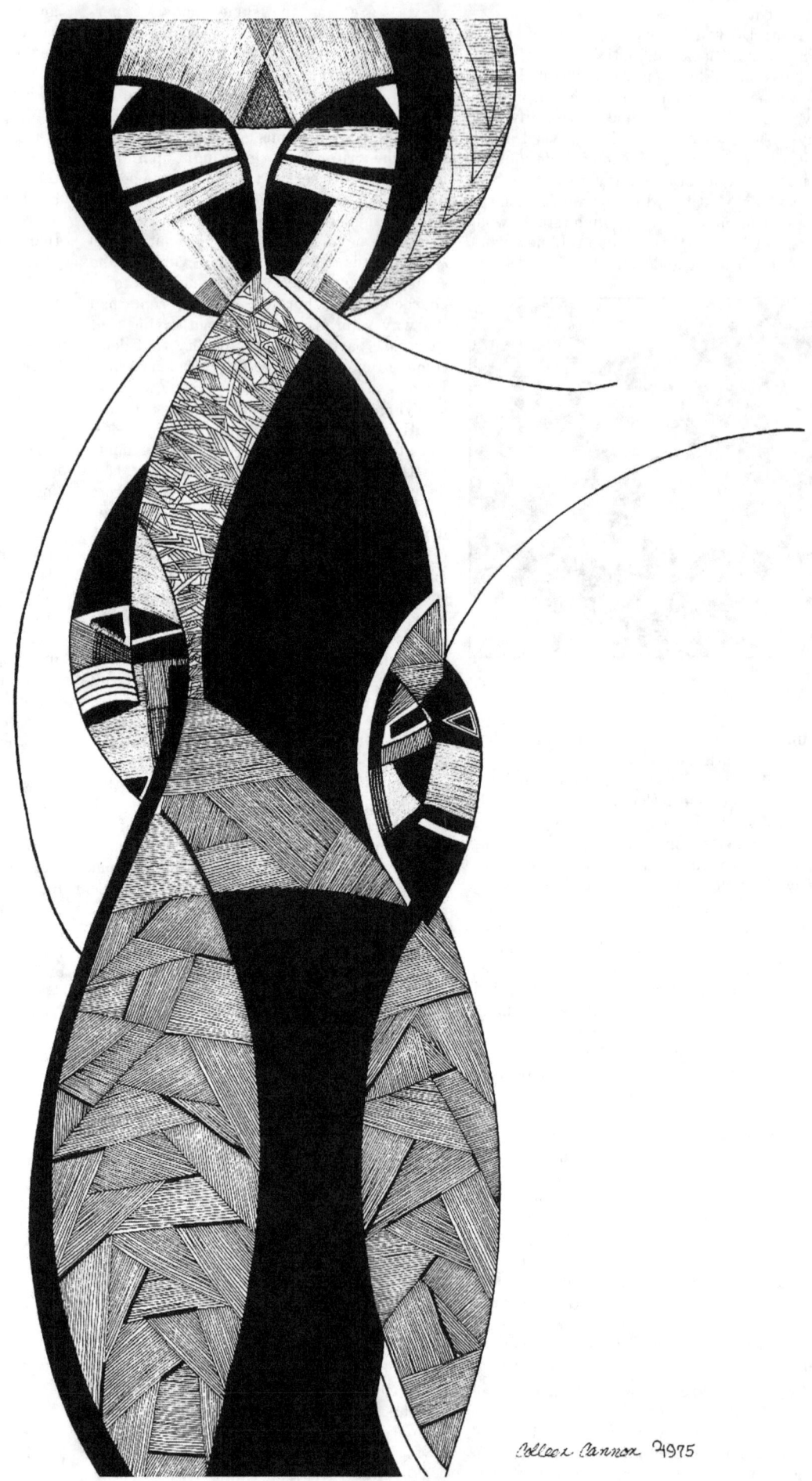

Colleen Cannon 1975

Conversation With A Native Son

interview
by
MAYA
ANGELOU

Maya Angelou: James Baldwin is an essayist, a novelist, a poet and playwright. He is also my friend and brother and teacher and pen pal. Since he lives permanently in the south of France and I live in northern California, we keep in contact by mail. Recently, we met in Los Angeles and had a chance to continue our conversation face to face.

Angelou: When you leave your house in France and come to the United States, when you leave your adopted home and come to you real home, what kind of response do you have inside yourself?

James Baldwin: I miss my family. I miss a lot of people, you know, who are part of me.

Angelou: Keep you alive...yes.

Baldwin: And a certain kind of speed, energy, beat, which only Americans, only American black people have.

Angelou: I know.

Baldwin: I miss that. You say, "my home." It's not exactly my home — it's kind of an asylum, it's a place where I can work. I have a lot of work to do, and if you are in a situation where you're always resisting or resenting, it's very hard to...

Angelou: It would take too much energy.

Baldwin: Well, you can't write a book. You can't write a sentence. And I asked my brother, David...we were driving through Harlem the other day — and I was in Harlem, I was living there...and I said to him, I said, "I wonder what would have happened to me if I'd stayed?" Now, you know David.

Angelou: I know David.

Baldwin: Because I mean, you know...because I also wanted to stay, you know, I didn't want to go. David laughed and laughed and laughed!

Angelou: That terrible, knowing laugh.

Baldwin: He said, "You'd be dead. Everybody else is."

Angelou: That's right. And you look around at your friends, long dead, lost in...

Baldwin: Well, David is forty-three. I'm fifty.

Angelou: I want to talk to you about that, being fifty.

Baldwin: About being fifty?

Angelou: Yes, but that's coming.

Baldwin: Neither of us know anybody our age. And my nephew, my oldest nephew is twenty-seven, knows one person his age. Baby, this is a high-priced country.

Angelou: Your family is closely knit?

Baldwin: I'm a very lucky cat.

Angelou: You're very lucky. I find myself very lucky because I've been adopted into that family. So, I find myself....

Baldwin: That's not true. You marched into it. You framed my mother, I saw you.

Angelou: Oh, I took her, didn't I?

Baldwin: You did.

Angelou: I'm going to talk about mother in a while.

Baldwin: Go on.

Angelou: But what does the family feel about you living in the south of France? I mean, living away from them without, say, an arm's reach...distance...out of arm's reach?

Baldwin: Sweetheart, you have to understand...you have to understand what happens to my mother's telephone when I'm in town; people who call her up to say what they will do to me if she doesn't make me shut up. You also got to remember that I've been writing, after all, between assassinations. I mean, if you were my mother or my brother, you would think: Who's next?

Angelou: That's mama.

Baldwin: It's extraordinary. The woman raised nine children, and every one of them...the difference between me and George, the difference between me and David, the difference between me and...

JAMES BALDWIN

Angelou: You and William.

Baldwin: ... and Willie, and all five girls. And though she was scared to death... no, really...no really, really scared to death.'

Angelou: You mean of your father, or after his death?

Baldwin: No, no. Scared to death of what was going to happen to us.

Baldwin: Because she knew something we didn't know.

Angelou: Of course, you couldn't then...

Baldwin: And there we went. And she never blackmailed us. And just, you know...when I went to Paris in 1948, it was such a rainy day. Mom came downstairs, and Paula was upstairs. Paula was five years old. The baby. And you can't explain to a baby, you know, why you have to do what you have to do. And she wouldn't talk to me and she was crying, with my mother. And the taxi drove away. And she let me go, she let... I think, I think at bottom, she knew how much — maybe she knew better than I did — how much I loved them. And I didn't want her to see me turn into a junkie.

Angelou: Or a prostitute, in any way.

Baldwin: No, in many, many ways. Go to jail. Because nobody could call me "nigger." I'd done the post office bit, I'd worked for the army, I'd been up and down those streets. So, now I had five minutes, and I had to jump to save my family.

Angelou: And they let you go.

Baldwin: That sounds very grandiose.

Angelou: No, no. But I know. Because I do know a story. I know that when you went to France, with Mother Baldwin and all those children, that from time to time...one of the lovely stories about your family is that, from time to time, David and George, or the older boys, would work with coal in the winter, ice in the summer, selling, and on welfare or whatever aids to some kinds of families, and still would manage sometimes to send you a little check.

Baldwin: Oh, I remember. I remember.

Angelou: In France! I mean, to think of a black American family in Harlem, who had no pretensions to great literature and so forth, as such...I'm using it in pips...great literature, and to have the oldest boy leave home and go to Paris, France; and then for them to save enough pennies and nickels and dimes to send a check of $150 to him. In Paris, France!

Baldwin: That's what people...well, that's what people don't really know about us.

Angelou: One of the things I think...I mean, I believe that we are Americans. It is true.

Baldwin: You believe it? I know it.

Angelou: Well, we are black Americans, we have our feet, our souls, our hearts in...

Baldwin: We have paid for this country.

Angelou: Absolutely!

Baldwin: That's why I'd never leave it, by the way.

Angelou: I know that. Never. And that's the lovely thing about...

Baldwin: At least, I've never deluded myself into thinking that.

Angelou: ...about that line that you can't go home again, you can't even leave.

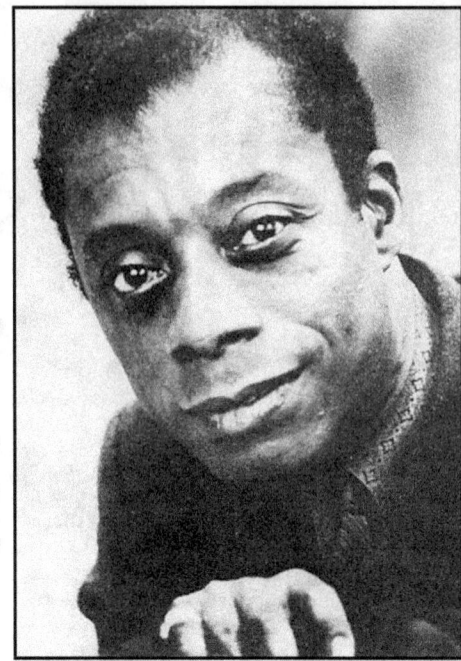

Photo by Mottke Weissman

Baldwin: You can't leave home. You can't leave home. You carry it with you.

Angelou: Of course, of course! And then create a whole atmosphere...

Baldwin: There are no Harlem barber shops...there are beautiful barber shops in Paris; there ain't no Harlem barber shops in Paris.

Angelou: No, I know. Or beauty shops, where you can hear who's doing what to whom, at what time.

Baldwin: There's not that speed, that beat, that fire, you know? You know, I owe my adopted country, as you put it, a lot. Because it left me *alone!*

Angelou: But when French people, or Europeans, ask you about your country, about the United States of America — or as I constantly say anywhere, it's what James Baldwin calls it, "these yet-to-be United States of America" — Jim, what is your response to the question?

Baldwin: I had to go to Germany for the publication of *If Beale Street Could Talk.* I was working very hard, somewhere...in Paris, in fact, in libraries and doing research. Right? And I wanted to cancel the tour, because I was into what I was...you know, into my thing.

Angelou: Yes, staying in your groove.

Baldwin: ...into what I was doing. I got back home to St. Paul and discovered that the USIS...the tour was for five German cities, and the USIS had broken its contract with my German publisher, saying that U.S. Information Service is not here to publicize novels and novelists.

Angelou: How did they have the contract, in the first place?

Baldwin: Well, it grows up in the normal way. The publisher — the German publisher, or the French publisher, for that matter... You know, if you come to town, and you're an American writer, you know, it's a kind of courtesy to the American Embassy. And they

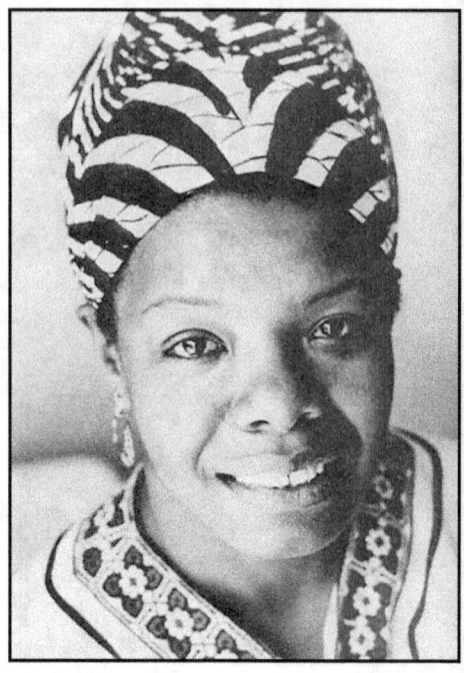

Photo by Jill Krementz

broke the contract. And this was all over the German press. In effect, I was being banned by my own government. That's not the end of the story. I called my poor brother, David, who'd just left, and said, "You'd better come back."

Angelou: "David, come. Yeah. Come to my..."

Baldwin: Come and take me to Germany. Because once I was banned, I had to go.

Angelou: Of course, you had no choice. Of course.

Baldwin: I had to go! And I went. Now, this is on German soil, right? And I was in a very difficult position, because the Germans wanted to say how much better they were than the Americans.

Angelou: To Blacks, yes. And to you, in particular.

Baldwin: And so, I had to say, "You got to remember...

Angelou: 1939.

Baldwin: No, I said, "You got to remember it all started in Europe; that's how we got to America. I know this was the Third Reich, you know, and I'm not going to let you congratulate yourselves about the disastrous performance of my own country, because I know your performance, too."

Angelou: That's right! And in Africa...

Baldwin: ..."As far as celebrated Negro problems are concerned, you know, if you really want to know what that is, look out the window. Look out your window right now, and see who's sweeping your streets. You call it 'the foreign worker problem;' we call it 'slave labor.'"

Angelou: They're Italians? And Arabs?

Baldwin: We left them fighting with each other.

Angelou: Jim, I tell you...your life. There are a million questions I have to ask, and I have to ask you to direct yourself to some...what they call "heavy." Young people have — especially young whites — have found that word, and they attach it to anything.

Baldwin: Yeah, they found the word, "beat."

Angelou: Yeah. You said something...a man had a question to you about homosexuality and you had a response to it, and I would like to hear it again, and again, and again.

Baldwin: I said...it's a weary, weary, weary question! I said, ' Homosexual' is not a noun; it might be a verb transitive, it is certainly an adjective, but it is not a noun. To ask the question means you don't really know anything about human experience, where it can take you, what it can do, you know? And if you characterize the world in that way, then you lock yourself out from so much." I've known boys...I swear to you, sweetheart...I've known cats — I'm talking about white cats, now, too, football-player types, who went on the needle...who went on the needle!...and finally died, because they were afraid somebody would call them a faggot. Well, all I know about human life — and I don't know much...

Angelou: Less and less?

Baldwin: Yes. When I was young, I knew a lot; now, I don't know nothing, which is a great relief. But all I know about human life is, if I love you, I love you. And if I love you and duck it, I die.

Angelou: Exactly, exactly. Well, then, you see, out of that I think is, for me...I see the nature of love, the ability to dare, to challenge, despair, and to dare to love.

Baldwin: Well, you see, you can't prophesize, you can't say, you cannot make a decision like, "I'm gonna fall in love with, you know...the girl that I marry...all that Tin Pan Alley jazz, right? You don't know! And you have to trust life. You have to trust life.

Angelou: Aahh! And when you say, "trust life," of course, that means all of it, the whole...

Baldwin: Yes, all of it.

Angelou: O.K. Then what does that mean about death? I mean, *about* death! If one trusts life, is death not in that circumference?

Baldwin: Well, I think...I think, you know, that the only way to live is to know you're going to die. If you're afraid to die, you'll never be able to live.

Angelou: Hey, hey!

Baldwin: And nobody knows anything about death, you know?

Angelou: Yes, yes.

Baldwin: And that is, also, just another word.

Angelou: For singing the blues.

Baldwin: You don't know anything about death, you know? When I go, I'll go. And where I'm going, I don't know. And it might be you know, beautiful, it might be nothing, it might be...you know, I think it's a cycle.

Angelou: I do. I agree.

Balwin: I trust my ancestors because I know — However this may sound — I know what happens to me when I'm in trouble; I know what my mother taught me, which is to love everybody. And when I'm in trouble, I listen to something. When I'm writing, I'm

listening to something. Because, you know, all this fad about being a writer and being a star and all of that — the truth is you become a writer because the day comes in your life when you have to accept that, you have to accept the fact that you're not a truck driver.

Angelou: Yes. Even if you loved it.

Baldwin: Even if...you know, ditch-digging I've done. You know, I ain't never driven a truck, but I can still dig a ditch. It's a division of labor in the world; some people can do this, some people can do that. And the people who produced you — which is what I mean by my ancestors...I'm a kind of poet, and I come out of a certain place, a certain time, a certain history. And the people who produced me, whether or not they always loved me or liked me or...they produced me...

Angelou: They produced you. And you're the total of that.

Baldwin ...and this is my gig!

Angelou: Jim, recently, you had a fiftieth birthday.

Baldwin: Oh, yeah. I'm fifty years old. Isn't that astounding.

Angelou: Indeed, it is.

Baldwin: I don't believe that!

Angelou: I don't either. But, I mean, you've made a statement about it.

Baldwin: I don't believe it!

Angelou: What do you think about being fifty?

Baldwin: I said to you, it seems very unfair because, you know, you're dealing with numbers, right? I'm twenty years away from thirty and twenty years away from seventy. Now, you know, that seems a little unfair, unfair in the sense that, "All right, here we go!" You can't go back. There's twenty years, you know, between thirty and fifty, and twenty between fifty and seventy; which means to me, finally, that I will have to hang around awhile.

Angelou: And it also means that you're closer, you said, to seventy than you...

Baldwin: Oh, I'm much closer to seventy than I am to fifty. But something else happens to you when you realize that. Something else happens to you. You realize that now you gotta use time. You gotta use the time. I ain't gonna live another fifty years; given my temperament and my stubborness; I might live another thirty years. No, all bets are off. But it does mean you gotta use the time.

Angelou: Could you stay alive, vital and productive, without your family?

Baldwin: No, no way. No way! If I didn't have...if I didn't know that was at my back...the net, I'm on a tightrope; I ain't no net, I'm a tightrope. Each time out...

Angelou: Yeah, out there?

Baldwin: ...it's higher. And yet, I got a certain safety, I really have a certain safety because we love each other.

Angelou: O.K. Let me just ask you this: How do you cope with success? And after that, if you want to weave them together, it's fine with me. How do you cope with despair? Despair, in front of the fact that the world is saying you're a success. O.K.?

Baldwin: I think...I don't know...well, in my own case, you know, in a paradoxical

fashion which I can't possibly explain, what is called success in my own case, right, came out of despair.

Angelou: Of course, of course. Life out of death, death out of life

Baldwin: That's how you learn to live with despair. You can live with despair. Success, I must say, is a little like, you know, finding yourself on a runaway horse, because you never see it coming. And, also, in a very serious way, it is not possible...it is not possible for an artist to be a success.

Angelou: Jimmy, would you say that again?

Baldwin: I said, it is not possible for an artist to be an success.

Angelou: Thank you.

Baldwin: Once you think of yourself as a success...

Angelou: You're finished. Finito!

Baldwin: Forget it, forget it!

Angelou: Because, you know, what I find is that you begin to believe your own publicity.

Baldwin: You begin to take your identity from other people.

Angelou: From something else. And you stop experimenting, because somebody says, "Well, when you did so-and-so, that was such a success. Why don't you do that again?"

Baldwin: Look, when I wrote *Go Tell It On The Mountain*, which is...twenty...God help us, 1952...I am fifty. But I knew something. It's very hard to describe. I knew...and *Go Tell It On The Mountain* was a success; you know, a young man's success, you know, a young man's book. And everybody fell in love with me and I was, you know, I was going to be the great new folk-lore hero. But I thought: No! I'm a writer. I'm not going to write *Go Tell It On the Mountain*. again!

Angelou: Is there any time in life when you start a project that you're not afraid?

Baldwin: Scared to death! I'll tell you about *No Name in the Street*, which, after all, was written between assassinations. I finally, as I say at the end of the book, had to reconcile myself to the fact that I was never going to be able to finish it. Because it was not a journalistic assignment, it was something I had to do. It was involved with the headlines, you know? It was a very public, in a sense, a document, dealing with a lot of public events. I finished it, that is I put it in the desk. My brother, David, came to see me, because David always knows when I'm in trouble. And he read it, he came down to the office and he read the book. Didn't say a word. Went back upstairs. And he said, "Have you mailed it, yet?" I said, "No." So, he went upstairs.

Angelou: This is in St. Paul?

Baldwin: de-Vence.

Baldwin: St. Paul-de-Vence, south of France. In the hills.

Angelou: Right.

Baldwin: And the next morning, he came downstairs and looked at me, picked up the book and said, "Ain't you got no envelopes?"

Angelou: Mail it off!

Baldwin: And he mailed it. He mailed it, because he knew...there's a moment in, you know, after all... I don't want to go into this, really, but you know I loved Malcolm and he got his head blown off, right? I loved Medgar, and he got his head blown off, you know? And Martin got his head blown off. I'd worked with Bobby K., and I'd worked a little bit with J.F.K., and...Lord, have mercy! And, wow! You know, it ain't nothing I'd done, you know — the typewriter keys, which saved nobody! And it took me a very long time, that's why I ended up in a hospital. It took me a very long time to reconcile myself to trying to be a writer again, because one is always *trying* to be a writer. I don't care what the world says.

Angelou: I know that. That's like trying to be a good Christian...

Baldwin: One is trying.

Angelou: ...a good Jew, a good Muslim, a good poet...

Baldwin: One is trying...trying.

Angelou: ...every...if you're eighty, you get up and you try to make that fit again, that cloak you put down last night. Exactly. So, I have no argument.

Baldwin: What David did, really, was to point out to me, in his laconic fashion, that I had to keep the faith.✿

Maya Angelou is the author of the following books: *I Know Why the Caged Bird Sings* (autobiography); *Gather Together in My Name* (autobiography); and *Just Give Me a Cool Drink of Water 'fore I Diiie* (poetry).

James Baldwin is the author of the following books: *Notes of a Native Son; Go Tell It on the Mountain; Giovanni's Room; Another Country; Nobody Knows My Name; The Fire Next Time; Tell Me How Long the Train's Been Gone; Going to Meet the Man; Blues for Mister Charlie; If Beale Street Could Talk;* and *No Name in the Street.*

and make any money. So now there is a great demand for Black films, they bid for these Black films, they fight for them. And for that reason you have at least two major theatre owners in the U.S. that are quietly backing Black films, so that they can have control over Black films and book them into their theaters first. And one of them happens to be a backing a film that I'm doing; they know that you put a movie in that theatre and that's money.✿

Letter to IMPRESSIONS

Impressions Magazine is endowed with a favorable quality. It is ethnic, thorough and rich. It conveys the essential elements of communication, in a fair manner (film, theatre and literature); it has supreme artwork coverage (some of the forefront pages were in tribute to a contemporary artist's work); and the information on the health crisis (cigarette smoking as a deterrent to better health and well-being, and its harmful effects to the lungs, brain and heart); all of which are all so absolutely relevant and deserve one's immediate attention. Impressions presents material in a soothing intellectual manner. The article on cigarette smoking has a personal essence to it, which is unique, and it thus helps to bring the utmost danger, treachery and waste of smoking into vivid focus. It has a spiritually elevating savor. There are many provocative and able Black artists and performers, circling in the realm of the creative kingdom and, as is evident, their creative capabilities are not enhanced enough through regular show business and theater operations.

I observed that Impressions devoted a decent segment of its composition to their syndrome, thus exemplifying the Black artists' existence and purpose. Many of the beauties and dilemas facing any race of people can be adequately understood if they are given ample coverage (in a historical and documented form). In this way, an appreciable portion of the differences are exhibited. The individual qualities, virtuously given to each race, can serve as tools to perform futuristic tasks in order to perpetuate culture. Impressions undoubtedly strikes me as the kind of literature that will continue to cite the best inert possessions of Black people, in addition to providing methods and possitive material to overcome the trials and trivialization of everyday life. — Lotola Johnson.

D'URVILLE MARTIN

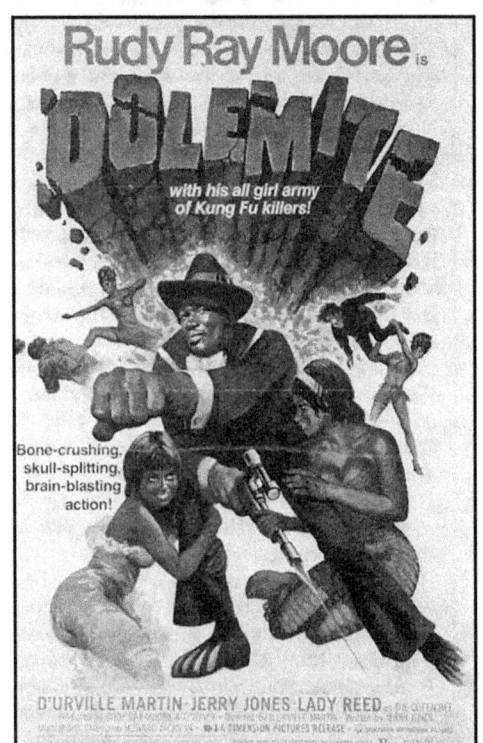

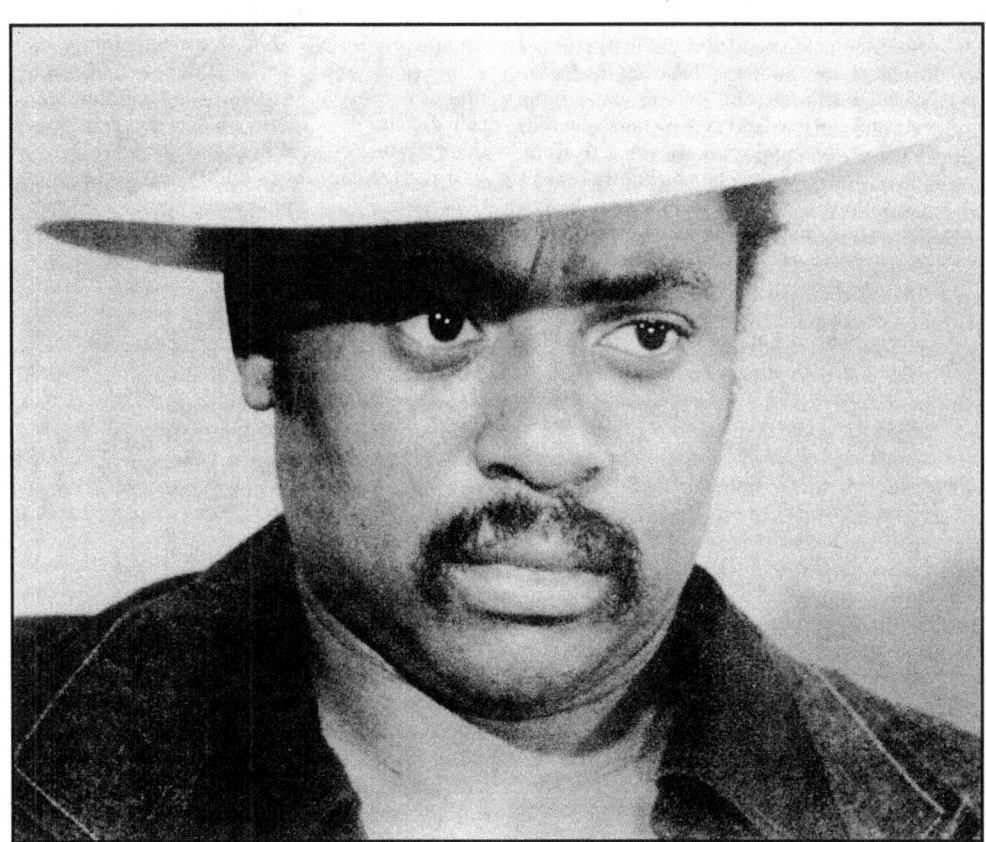

FACING THE
CHALLENGES OF
THE EVOLVING
FILM WORLD

D'URVILLE MARTIN

by Bob Bryan
Hector Lino, Jr.
Calvin Wilson

Impressions: D'urville, how did you get to direct and act in the movie *Dolemite?*

Durville Martin: I'll tell you this, an interesting story about how the money came about. I met the writer of the movie (Jerry Jones) in a supermarket in L.A. and he said he had a script and that a friend of his who was a comedian wanted to produce a movie and would I like to direct it. I just simply said yeah. So it turned out to be Rudy Ray Moore, whom I'd never heard of...and Rudy said he had his own money, $150,000.

Imp: Is that what it cost?

D.M.: Yes, $150,000. And I said ,yes,I would do it. At that particular time in Los Angeles there was an abundance of films made by Black people — produced, written and directed by Black people — that nobody's ever gotten a chance to see. It's unbelievable...and they waste their money making it because it goes nowhere. It has nothing to do with whether it's good or it's bad. I mean, budgets bigger than our $150,000; budgets of $300,000 and $500,000 in Los Angeles. So I thought it was rather sad that these Black people would put up all their cash on a film

and it would go nowhere.

Imp: Why wouldn't it move?

D.M.: That's because there is more to filmmaking other than just producing, directing or writing a film. The next thing is that you must know about distribution and promotion, and you have to have a certain amount of respect in the film industry. So the difference between *Dolemite* and all those other Black films that never made it is that I already had a reputation and a rapport with distributors. With *Book of Numbers*, when it was failing for about three months and not making a dime, I was called in by George Barry of Brut Productions to take over the supervision of distribution and promotion. I took it into ten secondary cities in the South and we didn't make as much as they wanted or, let's say, as much as they needed, but I did get them their money back. So from that, plus the fact that I also worked as supervisor of all Raymond St. Jacques' scenes in that movie, so from those two different knowledges I had acquired a certain amount of interest in knowing what I'm talking about in distribution. So when we did this film *Dolemite* I had to utilize my

background experience of working with low-budget films for white people on the production end.

Imp: Have you done a lot of that?

D.M.: Yes. One of them was *The Cool World*, with Shirley Clark. As a matter of fact, I eventually worked as casting director on *Black Like Me*, and that's when I got my first role as an actor. I hired me, 'cause I had faith in me... I gave myself a break (laughter) and it's been that way ever since. I had never worked as a director before. I worked at every other capacity you could mention, but never as a director. This is my first as a director. On *Book of Numbers* I had worked with a lot of non-actors; 90% of them were non-actors taken from location, and it was up to me to work with them, to prepare them for Raymond St. Jacques to direct. So I was used to working with non-actors and in this film we had a abundance of non-actors. We could not afford professional help on that budget; we couldn't even afford to pay me my normal salary. But investing my talents in that film, that is the only reason why Rudy and I share a piece of the pie. So I

13

was able to handle and direct non-actors. I could not make them the best actors in the world just like that, but I could make them relaxed and normal and to be themselves as much as possible, and my only thing to Rudy as a performer is to do what he knows best as a performer. He's a night club comedian, a party record comedian. He is the King of the Party Records; he's taken over from Red Foxx and he's going further than Red Foxx. For one thing, I think there's one other comedian besides him that sold over one million albums in party records. This is unbeknownst to anybody. As I began to get to know Rudy, I began to have a lot more respect for him, for his struggle. His struggle was the same as mine or yours. I mean, he's sold a million albums by driving across the country himself, loading them up in his car, going into the rural areas of Black neighborhoods throughout the U.S. and selling his albums. That is the reason why *Dolemite*, in 15 cities in only 5 weeks, grossed $2.7 million. Because of Rudy's appeal in the rural areas and my own appeal, having starred or co-starred in 12 films in less than 4 years. The two of us together sold tickets that no one ever dreamt that we could sell.

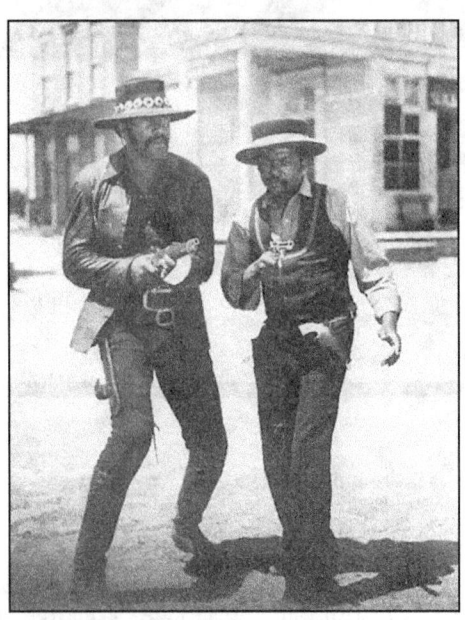

Fred Williamson and D'urville Martin

Imp: Distributionwise, how did you hook up *Dolemite?*

D.M.: No problem whatsoever. Fred Williamson and I were doing a film called *Boss Nigger;* everybody in town wanted *Boss Nigger,* 'cause out of the 12 films that I've done in less than 4 years, 6 of them are with Fred. Five of those films that I did with Fred were box-office successes and most of Fred's films that are successful are the ones that he's done with me. So statistically, they wanted that film. Fred and I wanted a gross deal rather than a net deal with distributors. The majors told us to kiss off; even though they'd call and beg us for the films, when we got there to negotiate I got the impression that maybe we had called them first

(laughter). So we went to a company called Dimensions, and we were their second black film that they've handled. The first film was called *Tough* or *Johnny Tough.* That was their first success, and when we made a gross deal with them for *Boss Nigger,* we became their second. So right away they loved me, loved me for whatever it is I am doing. They didn't want *Dolemite* at first, but other independent companies did, and when they heard about it — 'cause during the time we were trying to sell *Dolemite,* I was still involved with Dimensions in planning the promotion of *Boss Nigger,* and during the course I'd tell them that this company wanted it and that company wanted it — they got panicky and they said if you will give me *Dolemite,* I will do you one better than whoever it is that you're talking to.

Imp: What kind of financial arrangements do you have?

D.M.: I could say this to you, that on paper it is probably one of the best deals...better than Melvin Van Peebles with *Sweetback.* I thing it's a better deal than the deal that Fred and I made on *Boss Nigger.* It is probably one of the best deals that black people have ever made with white people on paper. I'll know for sure when the cash starts coming in (laughs)...which is the best deal.

Imp: How were you insuring the box office figures? Are the books open to you?

D.M.: The books are always open to us, but that is not the problem. You've got to have lawyers. You have to have accounting men to watch you because, in general, in any film — black, white, green or yellow — it is normal in the business for the theater owners to cheat the distributors, and the distributors cheat the producers, and the producers try their best to cheat the performers. I mean, there is a certain amount of that which is normal. We just want to keep it a normal rate (laugh) and not over (laugh).

Imp: What do you expect to do as a result of your success?

D.M.: Well, I've always have some personal properties floating around and as a result of this film...already there is a property that I've had for little over five years that deals with the integration of Blacks with the Seminole Indians during the time of the Civil War. There's a major studio talking to Yaphet Kotto and myself about starring and producing it together.

Imp: Would you want to direct it?

D.M.: The budget is too big for me to direct. I've had offers before to direct. Another attractive thing about *Dolemite* that made me direct it is that the risk was very little at that budget. I knew that I could sell it and not worry. Because in this business, if you do a film, particularly if you're black, it has to make money. If it doesn't, you don't get a second chance, and if you're Black, not only does your first film have to make money, but your third, fourth, fifth and sixth too. You don't have the opportunities that white boys have of failing and continuing. So I felt the offers that came my way with budgets like $500,000...forget it... you know, as my first directorial venture.

Imp: How long do you expect *Dolemite* to remain in circulation?

D.M.: I guess the rest of year...for a couple of years. You have first, second, third and fourth runs. Right now it is a box-office success.

Imp: In which cities is it playing?

D.M.: Chicago, Detroit, Cleveland, Philadelphia, Houston, Dallas, Jacksonville and Atlanta — we went to Atlanta first. I was afraid of Atlanta because several Black films have premiered in Atlanta and died.

Imp: Do you know why that happened?

D.M.: I really don't know why that happens. The only thing that I could say was that ours had what theirs didn't have, which was certain ingredients that do not necessarily make sense. But certain ingredients in the film...everyone seems to like the action in the film, and they also seem to love the poetic ghetto expressions in the film, which are done honestly. It was a surprise but it was a challenge. I said, if we could crack Atlanta...let's try Atlanta first. Definitely in the South and the rest of the country, I have to say that Rudy's appeal in the rural areas and my own appeal helped to get us over because of them having seen me in so many films. What I found out personally when I went to promote *Book of Numbers* was that, in the areas between New York and Los Angeles, I was like Elvis Presley.

Imp: It must have taken you out...

D.M.: Yeah. When I went to Montgomery, Alabama they mobbed me. I had a police escort and everything, all that kind of stuff (laughter). George Wallace had never seen a film that I'd ever done but, based on the reaction to me, he came and made me an Honorary Lieutenant-Colonel of the State Militia, Good Will Ambassador of Alabama, and Chief of Police of Montgomery, Alabama for a day. I ran all the red lights that I wanted to and never got a ticket (laughter). And when I went to Baton Rouge, the governor of Louisiana had heard about George and he made me a colonel (gonna do me one better) on his personal staff, not Honorary Colonel, but on his personal staff. So I have all these kinds of awards and everything, which I intend to use in making films in those cities, because I want goods and services for free.

Imp: In terms of today's commercial market for Black films, what do you think is the successful working formula?

D.M.: It's changing all the time. Happily, with the success of films like *Cooley High, Claudine,* and *Cornbread, Earl and Me,* it's changing all the time. I'm very happy about that. The saddest thing to me was when I was in cities like Detroit, where 5 films opened on the same day, including *Dolemite,* and opening night we had a line around the block to see the film and *Cornbread, Earl and Me* only had 9 people in there, and the only other film that had a line around the block — and they made more money than we did in that particular town — was *Mandingo.* That pissed me off that a film like *Mandingo*... I would rather *Cornbread, Earl and Me* make it; if a film's going to make more money than me, let it be *Cornbread, Earl and Me* and not *Man-*

dingo. In 1963, I think it was, they did *Mandingo* on Broadway. They could not find one Black person here in N.Y. to even audition for that, even as a play. That included Godfrey Cambridge, and he was working as a cab driver. Raymond St. Jacques, you name it, Roscoe Lee Brown, Cecily Tyson, James Earl Jones, myself would not even audition. They had to hire blacks from out of town. And it only lasted 2 days. We decided not to picket it on opening night and give it that kind of play. So it lasted 2 days, thank God. I was just amazed and appalled that they were going to do it as a film. I could not understand this. At the time, Fred and I were doing *Boss Nigger* and they approached Fred for one of the leads. Fred said he would do it gladly for two and one-half million dollars! (laughter)

Imp: So they changed their minds?

D.M.: Make no mistake about Fred. There's a lot going on that a lot of people don't know about whatsoever, in terms of performers. Black exploitation films have opened up films, everybody knows that. But what they don't know, to give you an example, years ago Black stuntmen could not get into the Stuntmen's Union. They might have had one or two, that was it, and now what happened was that the black stuntmen formed their own union. The first job they ever got was a film that I helped co-produce called *The Final Comedown*, starring Billy Dee Williams, Raymond St. Jacques and myself — that was their first job. You see, with the advent of what they call "Blaxploitation" films, black stuntmen are now working and white stuntmen are out of work, and not only that, but they are independent. Now the white stuntmen's union wants them to join, but they don't want to join. They're on their own and they're working all over the country; they're working all over the world. See, these are the positive things of what we call "Blaxploitation" films. I hate that term because that's preaching a separatism to me and it's not healthy financially. Films have to appeal to everybody, white, black, green or yellow...I don't care. I mean, I enjoyed Edward G. Robinson and James Cagney in *Public Enemy No. 1* and *Little Caesar* and all that because they dealt with gangsters, and I identified with it in that way 'cause Blacks weren't playing those kinds of cats that I saw in my neighborhood, see so...(laughter). I related to that, and I don't see why white kids can't relate to it also. It's healthier financially.

Imp: What kind of film is *Dolemite?* We talk about Black exploitation and we talk about Black films taking another direction...

D.M.: *Dolemite* is just an entertainment film with a lot of action. It's an escapist kind of film.

Imp: Was that conscious on your part?

D.M.: Yes, it's conscious on my part. It's conscious on Rudy's part and the writers' part...everybody involved. For me, personally, these are the kinds of films I like to see when I'm depressed (laughter). I like to go to the movies and see a lot of heads being whipped, you know. It's a film for escapism and to dream with. For most people, escapist-

type films mean *The Wizard of Oz. The Wizard of Oz* doesn't turn me on at all. The only thing about *The Wiz* that turns me on are a couple of ladies. But I'm grateful and happy for Black success. I realize now, because I'm part of it, that it is very, very important that every Black attempt made in show business be a success. Because this man's success over there opens up doors for that man over there, even though they're unrelated or doing it separately and all that makes it easier for the next guy. That's why the next generation that comes up after us will be doing a lot better than we are...will reach more heights. I'm optimistic about that. Sidney Poitier's struggle was much harder than my struggle, 'cause he came up when they only allowed one at a time. So the competition was a lot heavier. And now the doors are open for many more than just one. Sidney just happens to be the only one whose situation is comparable to a white situation, financially.

Imp: As an actor turned director, what is it that you want to say in your films?

D.M.: Each film will say a different thing. I don't want to preach to anybody in film. I really do not. I just want entertainment, but in the course of entertainment I will slip my zingers in. But I will not preach or anything. I don't believe in it myself. So if someone else wants to do it, fine. Let someone else do the preaching. Film is a visual thing, not a verbal thing like plays. Most writers, in their first screenplays, write a lot of dialogue and exposition. You don't need that in film, but you need it in a play because you're limited to a small area. So in film you can go to N.Y. and L.A. You have a broader area in which to tell your story. The film about the Blacks and Seminole Indians, there is no preaching in it, but when you see them together you don't have to any talking and they're fighting the man and they're winning. The Seminole Indians never signed a peace treaty, and they're winning. What is there to say? Ain't no talking there, all you do is enjoy the action and entertainment that's involved. The love story between the Blacks and the Blacks, the Blacks and the Seminoles, and the Seminoles and the Seminoles, and the action in-between. You just sit there and enjoy and at the same time you're seeing something that you've never seen before. I have another project that I'm trying to get off. It's a Black version of *Blazing Saddles* and I have Max Julien and Richard Pryor committed to star in it. I'm trying to raise the money to do that, and it's written by Ismael Reed.

These are the things that I'd like to do and I'm in the process of raising money for these things. I've been trying to do it for 5 or 6 years. When I present a property to the powers that be, to the money structure, the people who finance, I submit the things that are to my taste and the things which I consider are a piece of shit to put the money in. The things which are a lower budget, are a lower risk. But on these films I will not, cannot sacrifice budget, but I expect to get good quality out of it, if I have the right amount of money.

Imp: Do you want to direct it?

D.M.: Well, I at least want to produce it. If in the course of the next two years, I graduate as a director to bigger budget films, fine. But I want to make sure as a producer that the films come off properly and right...of good quality. I am not a genius and whatnot. Right now I'll probably direct a few more films, the next one will be $250,000 and the next one after that will be $500,000. If by that time I have not raised enough money to produce those other films, I probably will direct it. But if the money comes in now, I will hire a more reputable director to do it, who I have confidence in, who will do a good job and make it look like it's worth some money.

Imp: Who are some of the people open to young filmmakers to negotiate film deals?

D.M.: They're open to young filmmakers on a financial basis and how much money they can make out of you. The best possible deal is where you give them one-third and you keep the rest and they pick up your negative cost, meaning if the film cost you $500,000 they give you $500,000 upon the completion of the film. That is one of the best deals, because you're paying back your investors from the top. The rest is all gravy, if it makes any money.

Imp: Who are some of the more liberal companies?

D.M.: The independents. Any independent company is more liberal than a major studio. Major studios are by and large snobs. You have to be a Super Star or white to get a good deal. They're in the business to make money and they're not in the business to help you make any money. If it was up to them, they would like for these Black films to stop being made. They would like for what the Black critics of Black films are saying to come true. Because what would happen is that there would be less Black films, less Black employment and more white employment. Right now there are more unemployed white folk than ever before and more Black people are working than ever before in the movie business. So if it was up to them, they would be in total agreement with the Black critics of film. What the Black critics of film do not understand is that that would limit radio advertisement and a lot of areas would go down that people don't realize. So what I say to Black critics is, look at your white counterpart, look at his salary and look at yours and you'll understand that you're in the same position as this brother who sweat his balls to get something off the ground and out there in the public and make some money. There's no difference at all, we're all under the same hamlet and I don't feel right fighting a face that's just like mine, you know. I get leary of it but I'm aware of it, it's cool, I will deal with it and I will continue on. It gets tiresome sometimes, because the powers that be...your fight against them is an indirect fight. It's an indirect fight, you don't hear or see your enemy, but you know that there's a lot on you, that there's something blocking you. It's invisible and the only thing that's visible is a face that's similar to yours and it turns a lot of people in the business off on their own people...they say f-—k the ni-—a! Go with whitey because, as far as they see, whitey's patting them on the back. They're saying, yeah, you're a good ni-—a and we're going to help you, but they don't look at the splitting of the pieces of the pie.

Imp: Are you thinking of putting together some kind of distribution unit yourself at some point, or is that in your opinion a necessary reality for Black people?

D.M.: In order to have some control over the business, it's not in just producing, it's in distribution and exhibiting, because they do control that and that is where most of the money is made. It would cost me too much money to go into distribution myself; it takes an awful lot of money. You have an attempt, *Third World Cinema* is the biggest attempt, and it's nothing more than that, an attempt. 'Cause if you look at the films that they've done, it is in association with a major studio, because they do not have the proper cash to distribute a film the way it should be. Distributionwise, they have to eventually go with a major, and that's what you see on the screen. It's a nice idea, but it takes an awfully large amount of money.

Imp: As a director, what were some of the main problems that confronted you in directing *Dolemite?*

D.M.: As a director on a low budget film, what you see are my compromises for what I'd do if I had the money to do it properly. The ingenious thing about a film like this is being able to substitute quickly. Maybe there are shots where your crew — 'cause you can't afford the best crew in the world — is too slow, so you scratch that shot and do a substitute shot whereby they can shoot much more quickly and at the same time maintain the same ideal theme that you originally want, to some degree. With low-budget films you are substituting; you're compromising through-out and you have a limited amount of time. You cannot go a whole year like *Jaws* did to make a film. You don't have that kind of luxury. There is no luxury in a low-budget film. You have to go to the basics in making a film in the low-budget style. It's like a watch, it only takes so much diamond and gold for a watch to operate properly. The rest is just luxury and when you have 2 million dollars, you have a lot of luxury. The only luxury that I had on this film was auditioning 15 amazon ladies (laughter). That was my only luxury! A lot of times in low-budget films you luck up on some unique and interesting ideas and ways of doing things that you would not go through because you could affort to do it the standard way of doing things. The training, for me, was beautiful. Also, in the low-budget film everybody involved is more important. I don't care what position you worked in, you feel that you have done somethin' to make that; that without you, that it would not have been made. And it's all true! You have that love for a film, as opposed to a bigger budget film where you don't have that. In a big budget, you have union problems, where this guy cannot pick up this chair because it ain't his union and stuff and like that and it's impersonal. But a low-budget film has got to be personal and everybody's involved in it, down to the last totem pole. You have to do more than just one job. You do whatever's necessary to get the job completed.

Imp: There are some Black filmmakers who say, "I'm not going to get involved with the whole exploitation film thing because I believe that film should be of this or that quality." Yet there are a lot of filmmakers who're getting their thing off and their films fall within the genre of being "Blaxploitation" films. What do you think of those filmmakers who want to put out that quality film but, because of economics, can't?

D.M.: I'm suspicious of those Black filmmakers who say that they don't want to do any "Blaxploitation," and are starving. I'm suspicious of them, in that I think it's not that they don't want to, but rather that they haven't had the opportunity to...and if they did have the opportunity, they would jump at it.

Imp: What is your thing? Were you originally into film for the glamour or the bread?

D.M.: I was originally into it for the bread, and I did not know that I was into it for the art until I was in situation when I was starving as an actor. When I wasn't working as an actor, I was being kept by rich white ladies. It wasn't until a rich white lady in San Francisco asked me why I wanted to be in show business. I said because I want to make money, so she said, "Here's all the money you need, give up show business. I'll buy you a boat, car, everything, my place in Denmark and my place in France, etc. I'll give you money so you'll have money, so you can give up your show business career." And I had to turn her down. That was the moment that I realized that I was in the business for love as opposed to money. So I gave up that white lady and went into starvation (laughter). I feel positive about the business as opposed to negative, and I'm happy about the Black people around me in the business, who I know personally, that feel the same as me, measured by degrees.

But we've all basically wanted to get out of what we were already into. The compromises that we make to grab attention are so that we can say something. When Fred Williamson and I did our first starring roles in *The Legend of Nigger Charlie*, we had to plot and scheme like you wouldn't believe to get one black stuntman on that picture. At the same time we were being attacked by black stuntmen for not quitting the picture or forcing them into hiring more. This is our first venture; they don't even know if we're going to pay off yet. But what happened was, on the sequel to *The Legend of Nigger Charlie*, because the first made a lot of money, we had brothers on that picture. And by the time of *Boss Nigger*, that one brother we had the first time became the first and the only stunt coordinator over Black and White. Bob Minor is his name. Nobody had hired him in that capacity but us, where he was the coordinator over white and black, and he did a fantastic job.

We found out in doing the Nigger Charlie films in the same location that they hired a white wrangler and the wrangler would go to this black man, borrow his horses and charge us an arm and a leg. Well, when we did *Boss Nigger* we skipped that white man and went straight to that brother — where all the white guys go — and borrowed his horses and gave him the job as a wrangler. But we weren't able to do that until we were able to acquire a bit of box-office appeal, because they listen to money. That's why I say to most artists, hold back those "artistically honorable intentions" until you have paid off in the box office, because that's the only time they're going to listen to you. Only in accordance to what you're financially worth. That's the only time that they're going to listen to you. Talk too soon and you'll be like Scoey Mitchell when he had a series. They killed the series because Scoey found out that even though he had honorable intentions, no Black organizations supported him when he was fighting studios saying he wanted relevancy in his scripts. He said that in the thirteenth week. That's too soon! They bumped him. You wind up like him. No Black employment in that area, nothing. No progress, right there. So you have to be careful when to talk and when not to. You have to know that there are numbers behind you, because they listen to the numbers. When they're used to making money off you, they'll say, "Well, oh yeah." And it's all about money. The system is all about money; the corporations run it.

Imp: So you don't get hung up at all about being labeled a director of exploitation films?

D.M.: No, I don't. As long as I'm paying off. Eventually I'll get to do exactly what I want to.

Imp: Besides, I guess if there wasn't an audience out there you wouldn't be in business...

D.M. That's right! No one forces them to see those pictures. Those movies should be done. Whites have the luxury of having A movies, B movies and C movies. It's their choice. They have a wider selection of types of film to be made. What we're trying to do is the same thing, to have a wider range. But the choice, the obvious choice, is that it's easy to sell and easy to get money for. That's what they call "Black exploitation." But I don't see Black people with the same energy attacking white people who make these Black films and get rich. Now, they attack Black people who make these Black films and get decently rich, not rich.

Imp: Do independent distribution companies have problems getting into theatres because of the competition from the large companies?

D.M.: They do, but I don't think that's a major problem. But they do. The majors, because they make more films, can command that theatre owners cut short the run of an independent film and bring in theirs. They have more output, and right now you have a problem with Black films and Black audiences. There are not enough films being made to meet the demand. Once a theatre books a Black film and makes money, that theatre then becomes a Black theater. They cannot put Barbara Streisand in that theatre

Cont'd on page 12

ON FILM...

by Hector Lino Jr.

Sometimes we go to see films that speak to us, that touch us somewhere deep in our hearts. We don't always know why, but they take charge of our emotions and make us slaves for an hour and a half. It's not just the camera work, the acting or direction which creates the feeling that no one exists but you and the pop-corn. It's the clever gourmets' dish of our passions that entices us to the point where we will accept anything, anything the next scene offers.

Perhaps it's this single, compelling ability of motion pictures that unveils for us the childlike feeling of watching a world come alive once again. When there are moments of discovery from one scene to another, the film succeeds; when the images dance for us and we see those separate experiences which call on emotions pushed back into the far corners of our minds, our thoughts are transported to another level of human understanding, and, hopefully, we grow a little.

It is the language of the filmmaker that carries true expression, and language the cinematic delivery of our story, is the dialogue of film, a dialogue that should be spoken to one's people and thereafter the universe. For films to succeed at communicating anything more than jibberish, they must begin to inject a language into the minds of the people, a language that interprets cultural truths and provides the viewers with something interesting to look at. The language is, by no means, a blueprint to live by; it's simply projections of our/their world as the filmmaker sees it.

Unfortunately, Black films have failed Black people at this juncture. Our cultural realities and experiences never make it to the screen because they're exchanged at the producer's office for what some hip, pot-bellied, carnivorous dude thinks will sock-it-to- the ghetto-ites. Technically, these films are so bad it's difficult to sit through them and from all appearances they look as if they were made by paraplegic idiots, hurrying to get to the projection booth before the ticket holders take their seats.

With few exceptions, Blacks have not controlled the films that they have 'starred' in, and when they have, the Black American filmmaker has tried to satisfy the same specious desires that white filmmakers have played to since silent films. It should be obvious that we don't need any black Humphrey Bogarts, or black Clark Gables and Errol Flynns, nor do we need the black female super sex goddess. The white counterparts may be hip for white people, but Black people don't need to see anymore 'Super Cullid Guys' racin through the neighborhood in rainbow-tinted dildo cars, unless we can also identify the real authors of the pimp and hustler stories at the same time. Otherwise, what's the point?

As filmmakers, we have to begin to speak our own language. We have to talk about Mr. Brown, who runs a Fish-n-Chips store on Lenox Avenue and supports a wife and nine children, and about the old Black women, who walk around with shopping bags filled with rags and folded copies of the N.Y. Times in their jacket pockets. There's a wealth of substance and cultural information in those stories. The human interest angle alone has enough information to keep audiences coming back for more.

Blacks can no longer accept the excuse, "Got to make this film for the Man, then I'll make one for us." We really don't have that kind of time. We have to get some kind of facsimile of our heritage on celluloid before some adventure-seeking white cat decides to burn down the Schomberg library and rewrite the history books. More important, we have to educate ourselves about ourselves, and the commercial films don't have that kind of latitude. The people who get off making commercial films will continue to make them, and finally become incapable of making anything else except worn-out versions of impotent fantasies. If they're successful at making these monstrosities, the "one" for the people becomes less and less important. Because the insensitive producer-types who finance these films only relate to the trash that makes "all dat green stuff," so the people will never get theirs. It is, however, that green "stuff" from the pockets of millions of Black people that kept the movie industry alive in the late Sixties. Puff/ Black actors became box office, and Black people flocked to the movies to see themselves on the screen. There was a new Black image in movies, one that was, at least, less insulting than the coon films of the 40's, 50's, and early 60's. What Black audiences responded to in the first wave of these films was a form of language being spoken to them for the first time, a kind of dialogue between audience and film. A Black guy bucking the system, and getting over, despite the obstacles. It is the pathos of slavery revisited, the will to survive, no matter "how many different ways Massa tries to stop me," that packed 'em in the theatre in the early 70's. But the dialogue stopped because commercial filmmakers, directed by the dollar, clogged up the screen with to many paper tigers. And after two dozen pimp films and too many Pam Grier movies, the audiences dropped off because whatever cultural truths and cinematic freshness the early Black films managed to deal with got lost in commercialism. So did the language.

Black filmmakers have a special job to do. They have to become sensitive to Black culture. They have to attempt to capture our special scenario, the effect of the American experience on the Black lifestyle. They have to recognize the special value between two elderly Black strangers who walk down the street and nod knowingly to each other. Or the young brother who dances in perfect time to music coming from a car too far away for him to hear. The masters, Kurosawa and Fellini, have managed to capture their people on film. You know you're taking part in Japanese culture when see Kurosawa's work, and in the case of Fellini, it's the Italian experience that takes over your emotions for 90 minutes. Black filmmakers have to become masters at depicting their experience. They have to make movies about the Black Experience that investigate our lifestyle and take our existence in America to a level where probing never stops. If not, our films will suffer the same fate as Black writing; the people will ignore them.

Finally, Black films have to bring to cinema what Aretha Franklin and John Coltrane have brought to music: a definite style; a point of view; a language which has the emotional ability to carry you, like a subway car, from one stop of the human experience to another. Or, as James Brown says, "Make it funky." ✿

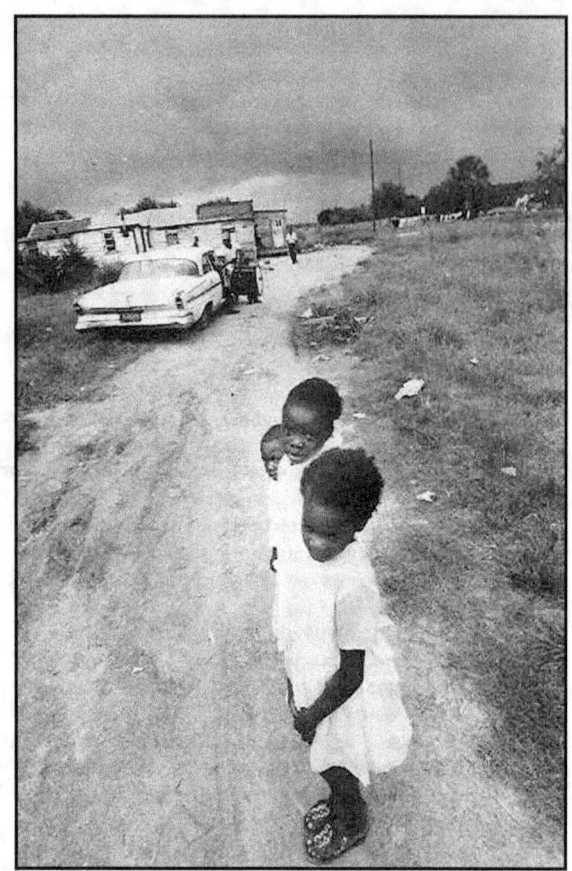

Ed Leak

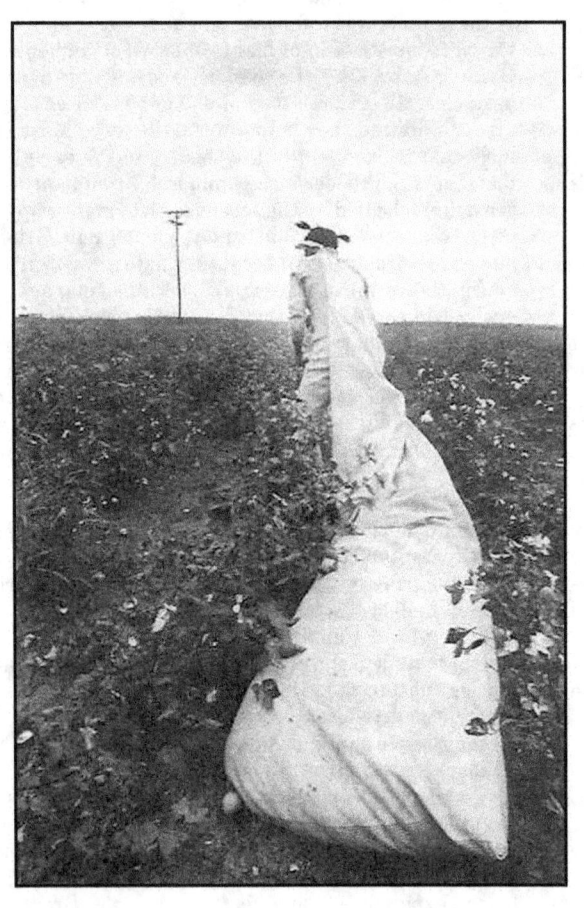

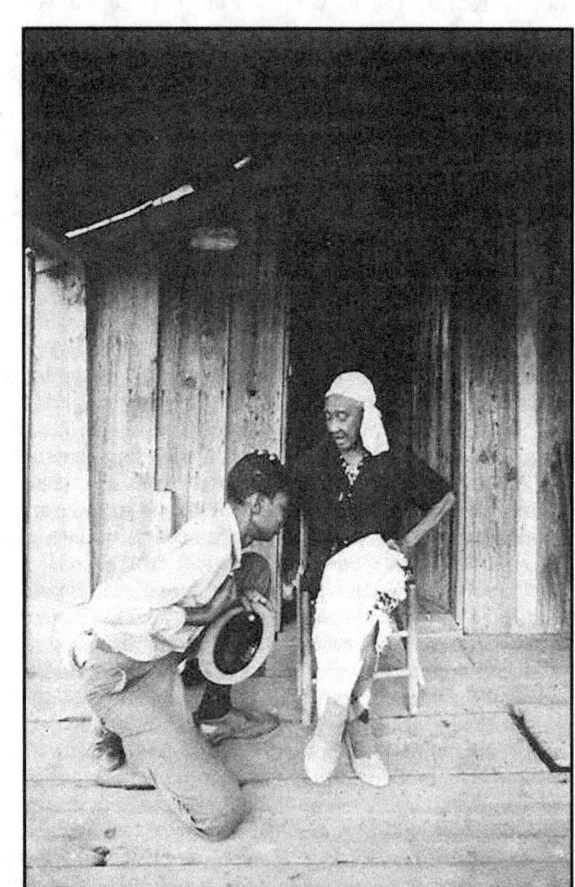

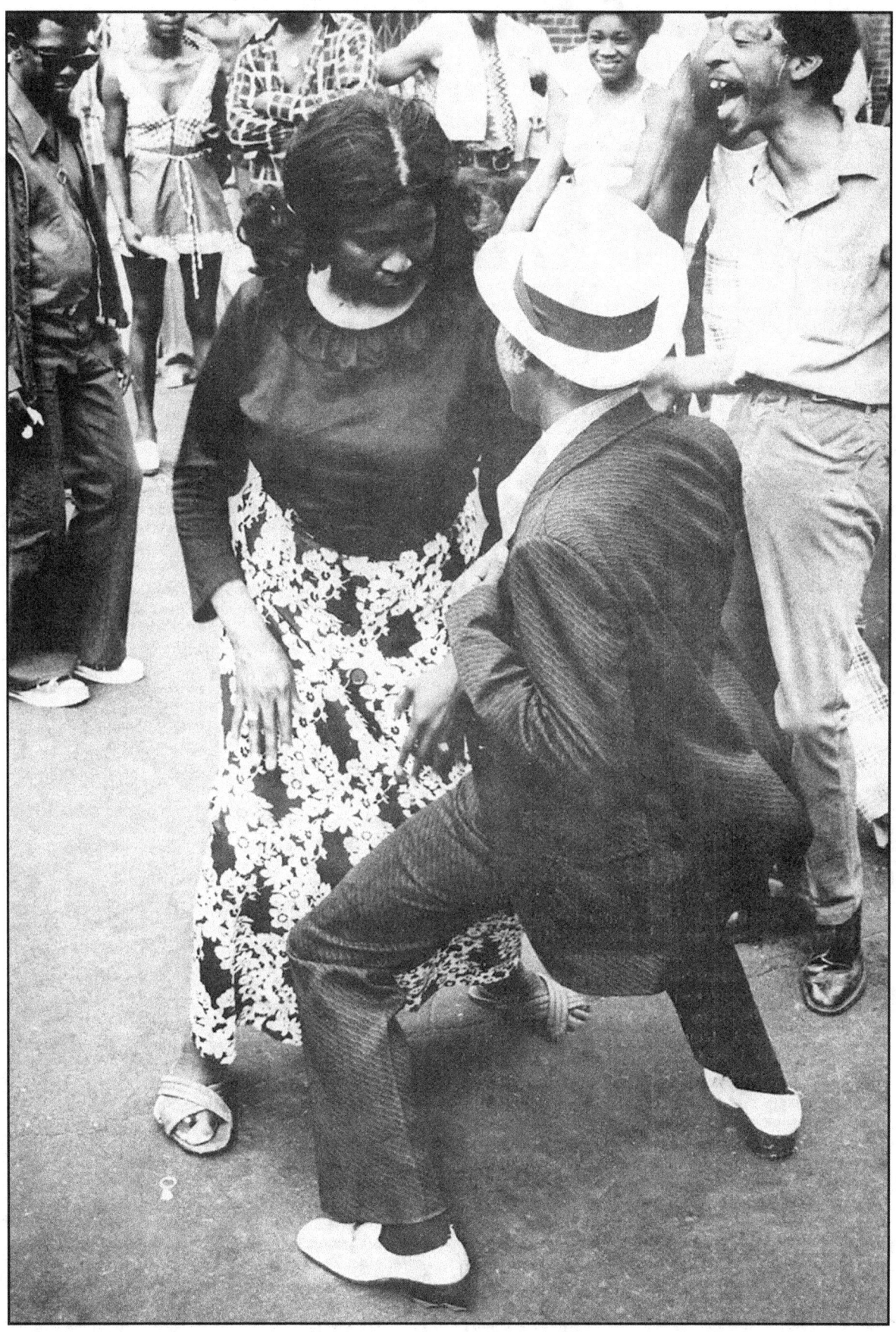

GOD'S TOUCH

A Chapter From

COLTRANE

A Biography

by C.O. SIMPKINS, M.D.

Demons no longer sapped his energy. He could now create freely. He felt that God had touched him and that he had experienced a spiritual awakening. Searching more intensely than before for the "life side of music," he began trying a new approach to chords. "I decided I didn't want to play the way I had been playing anymore. I wanted to unlimit myself some way. I had been playing straight along the chord — I wanted to play on the outside of the chord. In 1957 I was hearing some musicians playing what I wanted to play. It was being done, but I didn't know how to do it. So I decided to find out!"

It is difficult to know exactly what he meant by "outside the chord." He may have meant improvising from chords related to but different from those of a composition. Or he may have meant the extension of phrases in such a way that the end of a phrase would not be determined by the end of the time allotted to a chord. This latter possibility would produce a continuous flow of music.

During this period John and Odean Pope would see each other often in the various Philadelphia clubs. He told Odean that he had asked the Creator to enable him to reach out into the audience and hug them, as he opened his arms wide in an embracing gesture. He felt that through music much could be done if it had the right qualities and goals. He wanted to be able to strengthen people through music. John was very happy. He was writing, researching, and practicing with results that pleased him. To reach his goals he instituted a program of strict discipline with a schedule in which a predetermined amount of time was devoted to specific categories of study. For example, one hour was spent on long tones, one for listening to other musicians, two on chords, two on other aspects of theory. He would emphasize that minimum times should be set in the schedule and, furthermore, that nothing, not even visiting friends, should interrupt. He also told Odean of the value of a tape recorder in practicing. It enabled him to select the one of numerous ways of playing an idea that was closest to what he was trying to reach. With all the progress he was making he was still open to ideas or suggestions. He would inspire younger musicians such as Odean to continue working on a concept, if they really believed in it, no matter what it was. Whenever they presented him an idea with which he disagreed, he wouldn't be able to completely hide his feelings, but always encouraged them to go on, the only requirement being that they believe in it.

Other Philadelphia musicians visited him, such as Hassan, the pianist, with whom he discussed Islam and exchanged musical knowledge, and John Glenn, a tenor saxophonist, who would fix horns for other musicians. Glenn had developed a technique of playing two or three notes simultaneously on the saxophone, and showed John how to do it. John rapidly began practicing the technique to acquire a mastery himself.

John, Folks, and Johnny Coles would still practice together frequently, going over different chord progressions. John was very involved with a particular progression that would later be used in a number of musical contexts. One day he excitedly told Folks, "Man, I gotta tell you somethin'! Man, I had this dream last night that scared the shit outta me!"

Folks: "Yea, man?"

John: "I dreamt about Bird. I woke up in a sweat."

Folks: "What was the dream?"

John: "Man, I dreamt that Bird came to me and said, 'Keep, keep on those progressions cause that's the right thing to do'."

Folks, now also excited, shouted, "That's it. Do it!"

These progressions in their final development took the form of a formula which would be used to add more chords to music in which there were few. By using this formula he could obtain more color and variety in his improvisation, using a scheme that could easily be remembered on the bandstand or used when sitting down to compose.

In the evenings McCoy Tyner, then only 17, was a frequent visitor at the Coltranes. John would explain to McCoy many of his musical concepts as well as his discovery of the progressions, on which Charlie Parker had told him to continue working.

This was not the only time that John found music in his dreams. Once he was lying on the couch again with his head facing the back while Nita worked in the kitchen. Suddenly he awoke and jumped up to the piano. Nita wondered what had happened but thought it best not to say anything. After finishing John told her, "I'm glad you didn't speak to me because I heard something so beautiful in this dream, and I wanted to catch it before it went away."

She asked, "How did it go?"

"I got part of it."

John was commuting frequently between New York and Philadelphia, recording just as prolifically as he had since 1955. For Prestige on March 22, 1957 he appeared on an album entitled "Interplay For Two Trumpets and Two Tenors" with Webster Young and Idrees Sulieman on trumpets; himself and Bobby Jaspar on tenor saxophones; Mal Waldron, piano; Kenny Burrell, guitar; Paul Chambers, bass; and Arthur Taylor, on drums. On this recording, as well as many others during the fifties, his solos produced a rising spiritual quality of his music. The next business step was for him to obtain a contract and record under his own name. However, the recording industry was not nearly all that was to be desired.

Recording opportunities under contract were scarce and often resulted in compromise. Musicians were often told by a company representative to play whatever was selling at the time. Many musicians refused to record under such circumstances. The economic aspects were less encouraging than the artistic ones. Advances on record sales were very small, usually about three hundred dollars, out of which the leader of the group would sometimes be required to pay the sidemen on a recording session. Sidemen received a meager forty to eighty dollars per record.

Percentage of royalties on record sales were pitifully low, usually 3% but as low as 2% for the uninformed. One was doing well to get 5%. A musician found it difficult to meet living expenses, even on a record that sold well. This was not only because of the low royalty percentages but also because the record company reserved the right to delay distribution of the record for months, or years. There were other insidious practices. Sometimes the cost of the recording session would be charged against the musician's royalty account. Thus, if a record didn't sell well, a musician could end up owing the company money. It was common practice that the musician's compositions would automatically be published by the company. Therefore, any revenue received from playing the record on the air would go to the company, not the artist. An artist could also be cheated out of a portion of his royalties by the company's selling records abroad where it was easier to disguise the actual number sold. Regardless of the restrictions sometimes, not always, placed upon creativity, and the always exploitative state of the business, a musician relied on record companies to be heard. Hopefully, he would build an audience and reach a better bargaining position. This was the predatory nature of the business when John was offered a contract by Prestige records.

His bargaining position was poor. Prestige was signing many musicians at that time, at rock-bottom prices. There is evidence that Prestige was not very interested in John and that it was only at the urging of another musician, possibly Red Garland, who was a big seller for the company, that he was offered the contract. John asked his friend, Folks, for advice. Folks told him to sign, but with a one-year option to avoid being bound to the company. Probably in late March, 1957 he signed with the option and a $300.00 advance on each album. The fact that John's recordings from this period were labeled with Prestige as the publishing company indicates that his compositions were owned by Prestige. After signing he came home and told Nita, "It's no money. But it's a start."

On one of John's frequent trips to New York, he and Thelonious Monk, the pianist-composer, visited the apartment of the Baroness. The Baroness was a member of the affluent Rothschild family. She possessed a true appreciation and love for music and would come to the aid of musicians whenever misfortune befell them. After a gratifying nightclub performance, the musicians would sometimes want to continue playing. At the Baroness' apartment they could play through the night and have breakfast together the next morning.

While at her apartment John played *Monk's Mood*, one of Monk's compositions. Monk liked his treatment of the piece so well he asked John that day to join his group. When John returned to Philadelphia he told Nita, "Monk wants me to play with him. I don't know if I can do it, but I'm going to try." Being confident of his capabilities, she encouraged him to accept.

On April 12th, 1957, Monk recorded an album originally intended to be composed entirely of solo piano. However, Monk insisted to Orin Keepnews, head of Riverside records, that *Monk's Mood* be included with John accompanying him. Four days later John came from Philadelphia specifically to make the session with Monk. They did four tunes, *Nutty, Trinkle, Trinkle, Ruby My Dear,* and *Monk's Mood.* The first three were planned for another album. Immediately after *Monk's Mood* was taped, Keepnews, overwhelmed by John's solo, rushed out of the studio and asked, "What's your recording situation?"

John answered, "I signed with Prestige three weeks ago."

Keepnews: "John, I'm really awful sorry that I didn't get to know you or hear you earlier than this."

John: "No, I wish I had known myself earlier."

April 18th John was a sideman on an album with Kenny Burrell on guitar and Idrees Sulieman on trumpet. April 19th he was a sideman with pianist Mal Waldron and Arthur Taylor on drums. April 20th he recorded as a sideman with Cecil Payne on baritone sax and Doug Watkins on drums. On this session he contributed one of his compositions, *Mary's Blues,* titled after his cousin, Mary. Completely ignoring the negative criticism John had been receiving, the musicians were eager to have him play with them. The musicians always ignored the critics in forming their opinions of other musicians.

In the April 18th, 1957 issue of *Down Beat* Nat Hentoff reviewed "Tenor Conclave and Mating Call." The "Conclave" album was given four and one-half stars, and the comment,

"...Coltrane who has been improving rapidly never has struck me as impressively as he does here."

But "Mating Call" he gave three and one-half stars, writing:

"All six [tunes] are Dameron originals and are, in a sense, the prime virtue of the data...[sic]

"Although Coltrane receives most of the solo time, Dameron is heard on each number, and his playing is functionally conceived, harmonically sensitive, and personal...Simmons and Jones provide steady anchoring.

"Coltrane, who has become increasingly known as a result of his work with the Miles Davis Quintet, continues to improve, and his record contains some of his best work. As Ira Gitler points up in the informed notes, Coltrane comes in part out of Sonny Stitt and Dexter Gordon, as well as Sonny Rollins. [His fourth favorite is Stan Getz.] Like many disciples of the first three, Coltrane's tone is often strident at the edges and rarely appears able to sustain a legato softness, as Getz can.

" Coltrane has a feeling for variegated moods, but his tone doesn't yet display enough range and control of coloration when he expresses gentler, more complex feelings.

"There is an express power in Coltrane, an anapologetic projection of spontaneous emotion. And as Ira Gitler says, he is a 'searcher' with often arresting conception.

"Another horn — a gentler trumpeter, say — would have helped complement the not always attractive Coltrane sound and also would have illuminated the originals more fully in what would have been more substantial ensemble passages. But it's an album worth absorbing nonetheless."

Hentoff's statement reveals at least three common failings of critics of Black music and possibly music of any culture. First, there is the arrogance which blinds him to the fact that he has not mastered the saxophone, and therefore is incompetent to make statements like "Coltrane...continues to improve." Secondly, he confuses inability with honest differences, writing "...Coltrane's tone is often strident at the edges and rarely appears *able* to sustain a legato softness as Getz can." Hentoff seems not to have considered the possibility that each musician may have a particular sound because he likes it, not because he *can't* produce a particular sound. Thirdly, there is bias. Hentoff would like to hear a certain type of "softness" in the record. This is a value judgment which indicates shallow thinking, not unique to Hentoff. He states that "gentler" sounds are more complex and that "power" in Coltrane's playing as "spontaneous emotion" is less complex. Who can say that power is simpler than gentleness? Hentoff seems to have one standard to which he would like every musician to adhere.

In the May 16th issue of *Down Beat*, Ralph Gleason echoed Hentoff's opinion of John's tone in a review of a Miles Davis Quintet album, "Round About Midnight."

"The break at the end of Davis' statement in *All of You* is as close to a wail as he produces on this album and yet it is a very moving thing. His solos build beautifully to logical climaxes, and Coltrane, who customarily enters after Miles, seems here to have more of the melding of Pres and Hawkins and less of the bad tone which has been his lot up to now."

Gleason's qualifications on Miles' wailing, "...as close to a wail as he produces on this album and yet it is a very moving thing," and Hentoff's predilection for a certain type of "softness," brings to mind Barrelhouse Dan writing in 1940 against the use of prominent bass and drums. Each of these objections is against a distinctive aspect of Black music — wails, dynamism and deep sounds with drums. This continuity suggests that a cultural bias is at the foundation of these objections. Another continuity can be found, probably based on what people are accustomed to hearing, in the initial objections to the tone of innovators. Lester Young was condemned for his lighter tone which followed the previously established heavy sound of Coleman Hawkins. Charlie Parker was criticized with the same words, "bad tone," for his sound. John, also, in these early years received loud objections to his sound. Critics would like his tone on some tunes and abhor it on others. This was because he changed his sound to fit various moods. On one composition his tone might be mellow. On another it might be clear and high as if to clean the air and replace impurities with excitement. Audiences' opinions were still divided, ranging from absolute acceptance and pleasure to absolute rejection.

During his stays in New York John would visit Monk. "I'd go by his house and get him out of bed. He'd get up and go over to the piano and start playing. He'd play one of his tunes and he'd look at me. So I'd get my horn out and start trying to find what he was playing. We'd go over and over the thing until we had most of it worked out. If there were any parts that I had a lot of difficulty with he'd get his portfolio out and show me the thing written out. He would rather a guy would learn without reading because you feel it better and quicker that way. Sometimes we'd get just one tune a day.

"When I met him I started hanging around with him because I liked his kind of music. We'd already recorded one song together, Monk's Mood. I'd liked it so well I told him I wanted to learn it, so he invited me around."

On May 30th John moved to New York, leaving Nita and Toni in Philadelphia, to join him later. John stayed at the Alvin Hotel on 52nd Street in Manhattan. May 31st he recorded his first album under his own name, It was titled The First Train, and had Johnny Splawn on trumpet; Sahib Shihab, baritone saxophone; Red Garland, piano; Paul Chambers, bass; and Al "Tutti" Heath, on drums. Two of the six selections were John's compositions, Straight Street and Chronic Blues. Another composition, Bakai, was written by Folks. "Bakai" is the Arabic word for "cry," which Folks used as the title in memory of Emmet Till, the 14-year-old boy who was murdered by white men in 1955. Other selections were Time Was, I Hear A Rhapsody, While My Lady Sleeps and Violets For Your Furs. The last tune was suggested by the head of Prestige, Bob Weinstock. John accepted it because he thought it was beautiful. Weinstock soon realized that when it came to music there was no way to get him to play something he didn't want to. Straight Street begins with the baritone, trumpet, and tenor saxophone playing the theme. This theme is in the tradition of Charlie Parker and others in its phrasing, which may resemble the phrasing of the Yoruba language. If written syllables are applied to each distinct sound on the record, the similarity to language can be seen. The sound is deep and resonant.

Oscoobadobahdeeeebaaaa
  Oscoobadobadeeebabadobadebadeeee
    babadee babadeee bababaaap
  Scabadobadabadaaaaa
  Scabadobadabadaaahh
      Yaaaa bada baaap

  Ya da ba waah
  Ya da ba waaah
  Ya da ba waaah
  Ya da ba da waah
  Ya da ba waah
  Waa - da - ba - dwa yaaaa baaaa baaaa daaaa

On a soaring solo John enters with the high tone opening, brief moments of speech, roughness, tenderness — continuous ideas flow, each seemingly begotten of those that came before.

John chose another tune on the record, While My Lady Sleeps, because when the hour became late in a nightclub where he was playing, he would look up and see his lady, Nita, asleep.

Wispy strange slow
entertwinings of heated passion
the sounds breathe you
    breathe
    more deeply
        far
            away
                feeling
                    a
                SHOUT
                    a
            child's cry the trumpet
        joins John
            who disappears
                returns
            bearing a gift
            three notes
                three jewels
    Ruby, Sapphire, and Pearl

In mid-June Monk, with John on saxophone, Shadow Wilson on drums and Wilbur Ware on bass, opened at a converted bar in the Bowery section of New York, The Five Spot. As news of the music that was being made got around, lines began to form outside the club. Monk's debut there firmly established The Five Spot as a prominent nightclub. After soloing Monk had the habit of getting up and dancing around the club to a rhythmic sense that was all his own, and which appeared prominently in his music. The problem was that traditionally the pianist had the important function, when he wasn't soloing, of playing chords of a tune, thereby acting as a map for others in the group. In an interview John was asked how it felt to play while Monk danced. "I felt sort of lonesome, but I would count on the bass player. And with a guy like Wilbur Ware, he's so inventive. He doesn't always play the obvious. He plays the other way sometimes. If you didn't know the tune you wouldn't be able to find it. He's superimposing things, building the tension so that when he comes back to it you feel everything suck in. I knew the changes so we would manage to come out together. It's lots of fun playing that way. Sometimes he would be playing a different set of altered changes from those that I'd be playing and neither of us would be playing the changes to the tune. We would reach a certain spot and if we got there together we'd be lucky, and then Monk would come back in to save everybody. A lot of people used to ask us how we remembered all that stuff, but we weren't remembering so much. Just the basic changes and everybody tried anything they wanted to. Monk's always doing something back there that sounds so mysterious, but it's not [mysterious] at all when you know what he's doing. Just like simple truths. He might take a minor chord and leave the third out. Yet when he plays the thing it will be in just the right place and voiced the right way to have a minor feel, but it's still not a minor chord. I learned a lot with him. If you work with a guy that watches the finer points, it kind of helps you to do the same. In music it's the little things that count. Like the way you build a house. You get all the little important things together and the whole thing will stand up. You goof them and you got nothing."

Monk's inclination to do what he felt at any moment ment that John had to be watchful. "I always had to be alert with Monk, because if you didn't keep aware all the time of what was going on you'd suddenly feel as if you'd stepped into an empty elevator shaft."

By being with Monk, John learned much. "Working with Monk brought me close to a musical architect of the highest order. I felt I learned from him in every way — through the senses, theoretically, technically. I would talk to Monk about musical problems, and he would sit at the piano and show me the answers just by playing them. I could watch him play and find out the things I wanted to know. Also, I could see a lot of things that I didn't know about at all.

"Monk was one of the first to show me how to make two or three notes at one time on the tenor. John Glenn, a tenor man in Philly, also showed me how to do this. He can play a triad and move by false fingering and adjusting your lip. If everything goes right, you can get triads. Monk just looked at my horn and 'felt' the mechanics.

"I think Monk is one of the true greats of all time. He's a real musical thinker — there's not many like him. I feel myself fortunate to have had the opportunity to work with him. If a guy needs a little spark, a boost, he can just be around Monk, and Monk will give it to him."

On August 10th Naima and Saida, "Toni," joined John at the Alvin Hotel in New York. On August 23rd they moved to a small, sparsely furnished apartment in Manhattan near Central Park West. For a considerable time there were only a mattress for the three of them and a T.V., which John bought for Saida to make the move to a new city easier. The only other pieces were a refrigerator and a stove that came with the apartment. His day consisted mostly of getting up early to breakfast, drinking fruit and vegetable juices, lifting his weights, practicing his horn and thinking. He had developed an interest in health foods during his stay in New York. By the time he finished practicing it would be time to go to work at The Five Spot.

During intermission he would either go into a back room to practice or sit at a table with a worried look on his face, thinking of how he could improve his music. He would frequently try different reeds, whittle them down — trying to reach for something.

As far as the audience was concerned, the heights had already been reached. The lines kept forming and the group stayed at The Five Spot through most of the remaining year.

Archie Shepp, a tenor saxophonist from Philadelphia, then only twenty years old, came to The Five Spot every night. He had been receiving deep musical messages from John, as he had from Ben Webster, Sonny Rollins, Jimmy Heath, and other musicians of his heritage. Shepp was in New York on a work term from Goddard College, where he was studying play-writing. He introduced himself, "Hey, John, man. How you doin'. I'm from Philly," as Cats from Philly always introduced themselves. They talked briefly and John gave him his address with an invitation to come by.

Shepp came by — *early* — the next morning. He didn't realize that he had only shaken the man's hand at five a.m. and that playing all night consumed so much energy. John was sweetly asleep. Nita answered the door graciously, welcoming him, and went to the bedroom to wake John. He came out in his T-shirt. They talked for a minute and John picked up his horn, playing a cycle of fourths to teach Shepp. Shepp had his alto saxophone with him and played for John, who advised, "Shepp, don't let your hands go so far from off the keys. Keep your hands close to the keys, that way you can play faster."

Soon Johnny Coles, the trumpet player with whom John had played in Jimmy Heath's band in Philadelphia, dropped by. They took a walk down Central Park West, where tranquil nature and the clumsy city meet. John told Shepp that Miles and Monk had taught him much about harmony. He also told him of his experiments with the formula for adding chords, and of various ways to play chord progressions. It was a musical day. Each concept opened a world of branching concepts for Shepp, giving him much to practice when he returned to Goddard.

One night at The Five Spot, another saxophonist, Rocky Boyd, came to give John a message. Rocky had been sent to Miles, who was playing in another New York Club. Miles told him, "See that big fat girl up there? Go to The Five Spot and tell John that girl's looking for him." Her name was Margaret. Her parents had hosted John and other members of the Miles Davis Quintet when they played in Boston's Storyville. She was

only 13 or 14 years old, but her measurements were probably the reverse of her age, and she had a crush on John, running away from home to see him. Rocky rushed to The Five Spot and conveyed the message. John hid in the kitchen and told Rocky, "Tell her you haven't seen me." After Rocky spoke to Margaret, Miles gave him her parents' phone number, and they came to New York and took her back home.

Ray Drapper, the young tuba player who had seen John sick two years ago in the basement of the Bohemia, had moved to an apartment on 106th Street. He was overjoyed when Red Garland, who lived in the same building, told him that John had an apartment only a few blocks away. Ray was only 17 years old and attending the High School of Performing Arts. He was probably the youngest musician with a Prestige contract. He was displeased, however, with the way the company viewed the fact that his instrument was a tuba. To them it was a freak, a bastard horn. Ray felt that if he could get John to record with him, he would be treated more seriously. The next day he paid him a visit.

Toni opened the door. Ray was struck by the Spartan appearance of the room, and even more surprised when he saw the change in John, who told him of his spiritual awakening like a call to the ministry, and of being touched by God.

Ray would visit every afternoon. John showed him how to score his compositions and taught him the importance of breathing properly while playing an instrument. John was practicing, intensely as before, scales with numerous variations, intervals, harmonies, the upper register of his horn, playing two or three notes at once, and what he termed a 3-on-1 chord approach. He explained what he meant by this. "I could stack up chords — say, on a C-seventh, I sometimes superimposed an E-flat-seventh, up to an F-sharp-seventh, down to an F. That way I could play three chords on one."

While developing this approach, John was listening to an advanced European harpist named Salzeda. He owned a record of Salzeda's, "Transcriptions For Two Harps." For a period of a few months he listened constantly to Salzeda's recordings in his usual position of the couch, and went to sleep at night by them. Later, he bought records of other harpists, but Salzeda was his favorite. The music of the harp is sweeping and continuous like waves of the ocean. The music he created from the 3-on-1 chord approach, as well as other devices, was similarly fluid. Scales formed the body of this sweeping whirling fabric. These were played incredibly fast, with an unpredictable variety of accentuations, phrasing, and intonations. Wave after barrage after wave of notes woven...

The gap between his art and critics' perception of it was narrowing. His audience was steadily growing. Many of them were excited by the emotional content of his music. An indication of his gradual acceptance was given by the International Critics Poll in *Down Beat* August 22nd, 1957. John was voted second, behind Sonny Rollins, in the new star category. Critics from the non-English speaking countries may have been responsible for his high placement in this poll.

On days-off from The Five Spot engagement John would sometimes make gigs in Washington, D.C. He had no steady band, but would gather musicians whenever a job came up. At one of his performances he met a group from Liberia which was close to the Liberian Ambassador to the United States. He enjoyed this group of people so much that he wrote the composition, *Liberia*.

On a night off John called Folks, who was living in Brooklyn, and told him that he wanted to see him. They took a long ride in John's first car, which he had bought while with Monk. He would drive it everywhere, even to a store only a block away. They rode to New Jersey without John saying a word. To break the ice, Folks interrupted the silence, "What you want to see me about, man?"

Very bluntly John answered, "Do you think I should get a band?"

Folks: "Hell, yeah! And when you get it, get all them saxophones lined up like that rich white boy. That rich white boy

Charlie Barnet. Play the tenor. Play the soprano, and for God's sake go back to the alto. Play the flute. Blow all them mother-fuckers, man. That'd be a gimmick, and you'd make a lot of money, John."

John, hesitating, "But I ain't got no personality like you. You know, I'm shy and shit."

Folks: "Yeah, but you can play. That's the difference. I can't play. I got to have personality to get across. You can wail. I can't wail. You ain't got to have no personality. All you got to do is blow that horn."

John thought this over carefully. In the meantime he recorded again on September 15th with Blue Note records, by "courtesy" of Prestige. On this date he had with him, Lee Morgan, trumpet; Curtis Fuller, trombone; Kenny Drew, piano; Paul Chambers, bass; and Philly Joe Jones, drums. Three of the five selections, *Locomotion*, *Blue Train* and *Lazy Bird* were written before he came to New York permanently. At the recording session he was told at the last minute that another selection was needed to complete the album. John then wrote a composition which he aptly titled, *Moment's Notice*. In this composition he utilized the pedal point device which he had employed before *Nita*. The theme of *Moment's Notice* is a happy and arresting statement. *Blue Train* is an eerie blues on which John wails with fire and a high degree of inventiveness. There is a sound throughout his playing that lifts your perception of feelings and of your surroundings.

In John's beautiful rendition of another selection on this album, *I'm Old Fashioned*, an extremely important device is revealed. Within a portion of his solo he plays with shifting accents, alternating delicately, his sound with that of the piano. A feeling of floating slowly upward is created. This same device of shifting accents is used frequently in John's later music, in high energy pieces, as sort of a signal to move the band as one unified mass in stepwise manner, to a higher level.

Toward the end of the year Monk became tired of working and disbanded his group in late December. Orin Keepnews, head of Riverside records had tried to record the group live at The Five Spot, but was unsuccessful, because of the great rivalry which existed between Prestige, which had John under contract, and his company which had contracted Monk. Keepnews asked Weinstock, head of Prestige for permission to record John. Weinstock agreed on condition that Monk be allowed to play on a Prestige record with John as leader. Keepnews reluctantly agreed.

Monk alledgedly refused. He had been with Prestige before signing with Riverside and felt so bitter that he didn't want to record with them under any circumstances. While with Prestige, Monk was at a low point in his career. His cabaret card had been cancelled, and he was not allowed to play in any nightclub in New York. He felt that Prestige dealt with him unfairly during this period. When he left the company, he allegedly owed *them* money. Therefore, much of the historic music of this period was never recorded.

Miles Davis asked John to rejoin his group. John accepted and the group played in Chicago during the holiday. As 1957 ended, further signs of John's increasing popularity with the public appeared. The first enthusiastic review of John's playing in *Down Beat* appeared in the December 26th issue. Dom Ceruli wrote the review of *Monk's Music*.

> "It's a tribute to Monk that within this intensely personal music, a soloist like Coltrane can develop a singularly personal style of his own, while fitting into the frame of Monk's reference. Trane's work on *Epistrophy*, for example, is about as fine as I've heard from him on record. In person, his playing is constantly tense and searching, always a thrilling experience."

Also for the first time John placed in *Down Beat's* regular tenor saxophone category in addition to the new star category. John was 11th in the regular saxophone category. Sonny Rollins was second and Stan Getz was first.

Nineteen fifty-seven was a year of transition for John. His spirit finally broke the glass enclosure that had mentally and physically incarcerated him. Even during his period of depression he had maintained his religious beliefs. But now his actions were at one with his faith, thereby creating an immense positive force. Through music he was free to convey strength to people, making them better able to sustain the trials and tribulations of life. While gaining impetus from his spiritual awakening and through communication received from his predecessor Charlie Parker, numerous technical developments began to appear in John's music.

Already a heavy practicer, he instituted an even stricter program to develop his concepts. His search for a "sweeping sound," his listening to the harp, revealed his interest in producing continuous music. Some of the concepts he was in the process of developing were formulas for adding more chords to a composition, the ability to play two, or three tones at once, and the 3-on-1 chord approach. Scales played rapidly and with numerous variations were an increasingly important component of his music. One scale led to another and another and another, making the vertical approach to music also a horizontal one.

Musically, and in general, he was wide open and continued to learn from Monk and Miles, as well as from many who were not well known, and even those less competent than himself.

One characteristic of Monk's music was wide intervals from one note in the melody to another or from one chord to another. This may have encouraged John to investigate intervals more fully. The use of wide intervals is a characteristic feature of Black music. Singers, for example, sing a low note, then all of a sudden jump high into what is called "falsetto."

Much was revealed in John's ballad renditions, in which he utilized fast-moving, rich ornamentation against a slow tempo, a heartfelt feeling, and a naturalness that could cause a listener to breathe in a more natural manner, with full even breaths.

Whether the music was at a slow or fast tempo, there was always passion in his playing. At fast tempos, there were zeal and towering strength of soldiers of the Zulu warrior Shaka and of Mohammed's horse riders who would die for their religion, and of the barefoot soldiers of Toussaint who smashed the best forces of Napoleon.

The coming impact of Coltrane could be seen by considering the opposition to his music. In the tradition of previous innovators, there were heated objections to his tone, or sound. Such objections seem to have presaged each musical revolt of Black music in western society. Indeed, other rumblings of revolt were being heard in the recordings of musicians like Ornette Coleman, Sun Ra, and Cecil Taylor released during this year. Several conceptual streams of musicians began migrating to New York because of the greater opportunities for recording, performing, and publicity. The business part of the music, however, was overwhelmingly exploitative, and though opportunities appeared colorful, there was only a wall of frustration at the end of the rainbow. These elements and others, made up the swirl of circumstances that John and his small family moved into, in 1957. ✿

Reprinted from Coltrane: A Biography, by permission of Herndon House Publishers. °Cuthbert Ormond Simpkins, M.D., 1975. For further information about the book contact C.O. Simpkins through the following address:

> *Cuthbert Ormond Simpkins*
> *Herndon House Publishers*
> *Suite 17D,*
> *25 W. 132 St.,*
> *New York, N.Y. 10037*

In my first article I dealt with the necessity of proper eating habits and the science of healthy living, then in the next article I dealt with the poisons in our bodies. Now that I have explained why it is necessary to be conscious of diets and what should be excluded from our diets, we can approach the subject of body purification through a cleansing and healing diet. After years of erroneous eating habits, how do we begin — where do we start — to cleanse our bodies? Well, it is a slow process that definitely does not happen overnight.

The first step is to consciously stop eating all unnatural or processed foods; they must be eliminated from the diet. This includes canned foods, junk foods, chemically-processed foods and all types of condiments. The diet will now start to be a cleansing diet in preparation for fasting. It will consist of the following foods: cheeses, vegetables, whole grains, eggs and especially dates, prunes, figs and raisins, which should be eaten freely. It will eventually be exclusively fruits, dates, prunes, figs and raisins.

This preparatory diet will last three weeks. In conjunction with this diet, various herbal teas should be taken daily. This is the second step of the cleansing process. These teas consist of various combinations of herbs according to the individual needs of the person. Some basic cleansing teas are the following: burdock root, bayberry bark and comfrey. These should be taken freely throughout the day for the duration of the three-week period. Of course, the types of herbs and their various strengths depend on the types of food the person ate prior to the cleansing process. Fresh clean water should be taken four to five times daily.

tain this pose for a few seconds and relax the body. Hold your breath while doing this pose. Do not permit jerks when doing this pose.

This next exercise is a good basic exercise that stimulates peristalic action and massages the bowels. Lie flat on your back, bring your knees toward your chest, and pant, breathing in short, rapid gasps. Roll on your right side, face, and left side, and continue panting.

These are just two exercises that aid in elimination. I might mention that exercises should never be done in a closed, stuffy room. Ideally, the best place to exercise is outside in fresh air, but a room with good ventilation is very acceptable.

After three weeks of preparation, with the proper diet and the aid of herbs and exercises, the body is ready for a short fast. The preparatory diet before fasting is necessary because when the body is no longer taking in foods, it must rely on its own vitality. This vitality depends on the condition of the body.

When poisons and obstructions are present in the body, it lowers the vitality considerably; this is why the elimination process is so important. When you fast, the primary obstructions resulting from improper diet are immediately eliminated. These poisons are carried away by the bloodstream to be eliminated thru the kidneys. This is why some people feel so terrible at the beginning of a fast; they have not prepared their bodies and the poisons and wastes are released into the bloodstream. If one has faulty elimination, then the waste materials which accumulate on the intestinal walls produce a condition that is conducive to disease. So before one fasts, the body should be relatively clean from poisons and waste materials.

FASTING
AND YOUR SPIRITUAL WELL-BEING
by Brenda Bailey

By the end of the first week a mild herbal laxative should be taken. This is the third step in the cleansing process. Since the body has started to cleanse itself naturally by the eating of proper cleansing foods, it is now time to aid the process by taking a mild laxative. Some that may be used for this purpose are: senna pods, fennel seed and blue flag root. These laxatives produce a cleansing and flushing of numerous toxins and mucous from the bloodstream and body. The laxative should be taken before retiring at night, with at least three glasses of water. The diet the next day should be nourishing and rich in vitamins and minerals. Food should be eaten in small amounts and at a slow pace the next day. A sample menu would be fresh juice in the morning 20 minutes after having a glass of water. Thirty minutes later, a mixture of wheat germ, honey and raisins should be eaten. The heavy meal should be a fresh, crisp salad or fresh vegetable soup.

The basic cleansing process is in effect now and the physical energy level should be increased. The next step in the preparatory diet is eliminating the dairy products, and the menu will consist of raw vegetables, fresh fruits and the eliminating foods of raisins, dates, prunes and figs. Again, I must mention the importance of drinking water frequently throughout the day.

To further aid the elimination process, the use of physical exercise and Yogic breathing is of great value. They not only aid in elimination but also increase circulation and build physical stamina. I will now mention some sample exercises that aid in elimination and remove constipation. The first exercise is a yoga pose called the Bow Pose. Lie face down. Relax your muscles. Now, bend legs over thighs. Firmly catch hold of the right ankle with the right hand and the left ankle with the left hand. Raise your head, body and knees by tugging at the legs with the hands so that the whole burden of the body rests on the abdomen and the spine is nicely arched backward like a bow. Main-

The first day of the fast should be spent in quiet meditation or some creative activity. A glass of lemon juice, water and honey is good in the morning because it is cleansing and helps dissolve mucous (built-up waste). At least seven glasses of water should be taken throughout the day. If you drink only water during the fast, the human mechanism cleanses itself, the same way you would press out a dirty water sponge. The dirty water in the body is composed of waste and poisons that must pass through the circulation until dissolved enough to pass through the kidneys. The tissues, in contracting, squeeze out the poisons and mucous. This is why fasting is the most natural body-cleanser and purifier. The first fast should last 3 to 4 days to give the body enough time to properly cleanse itself.

Deep-breathing exercises should be done at regular intervals throughout the day. Other light exercises also aid the body during fasting.

Breaking the fast must be done conscientiously. The first meal after a fast must consist of laxative-type foods, so they may aid in carrying away the released poisons and wastes through the bowels. The type of foods you eat after the fast depends on your diet before the fast. Fresh fruits and soaked or stewed prunes are good for non-meat eaters to break a fast. Raw and cooked vegetables are good for the prior meat-eater.

I have tried to give a basic understanding of the benefits of fasting; however, guidance is recommended for the first couple of fasts to ensure the optimum benefits. Every body is different and many factors must be considered before fasting. There are different ways of fasting and it is good to find one which is most suitable for your lifestyle and most beneficial to your body's needs.

In the next issue I will deal exclusively with the mental aspects of body and soul purification. Blessings. ✿

The author is now giving individual and group instruction using nutritional and astrological analyses. For further information contact Bob Bryan, Publisher, at (212) 862-1326.

MEL
WRIGHT

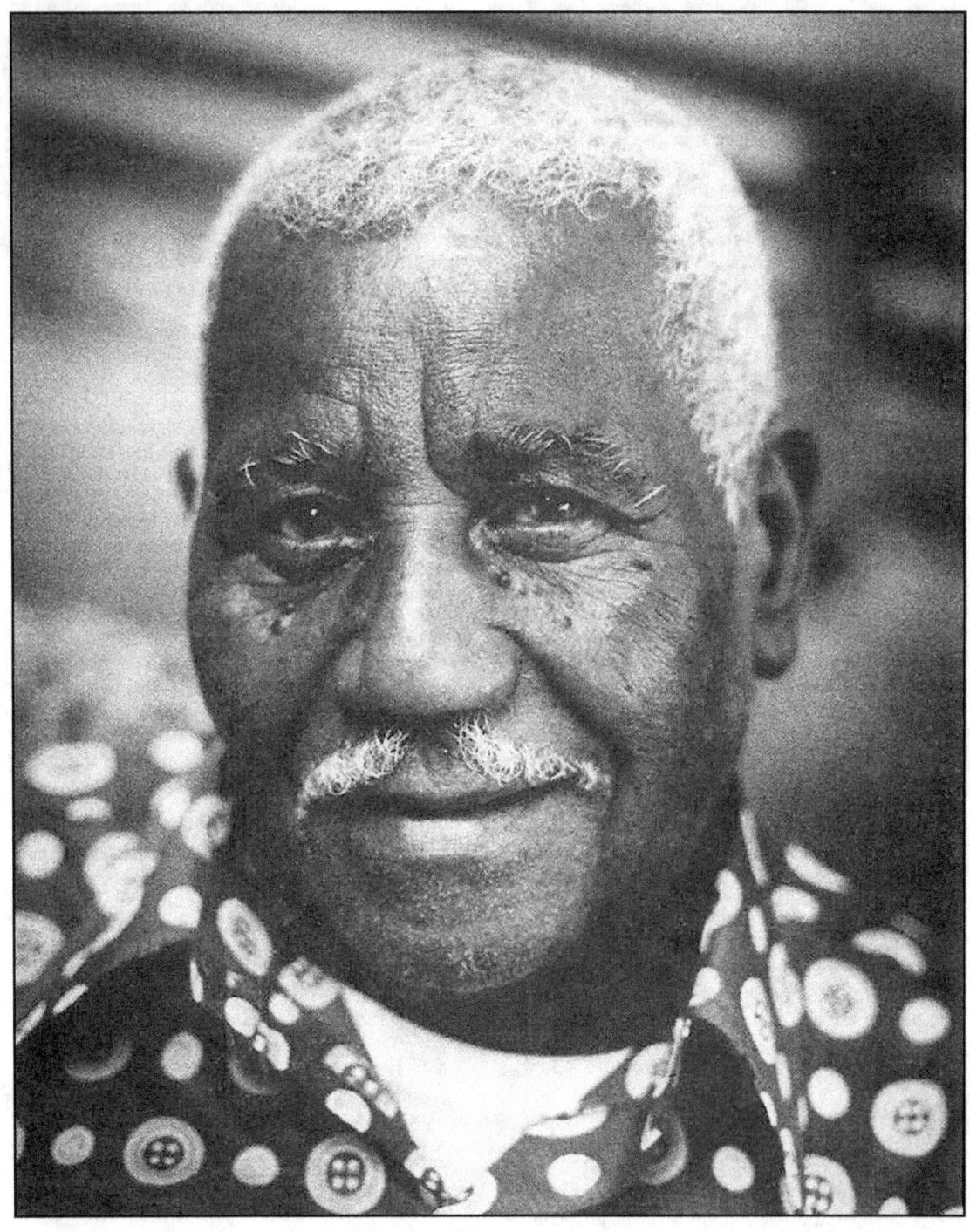

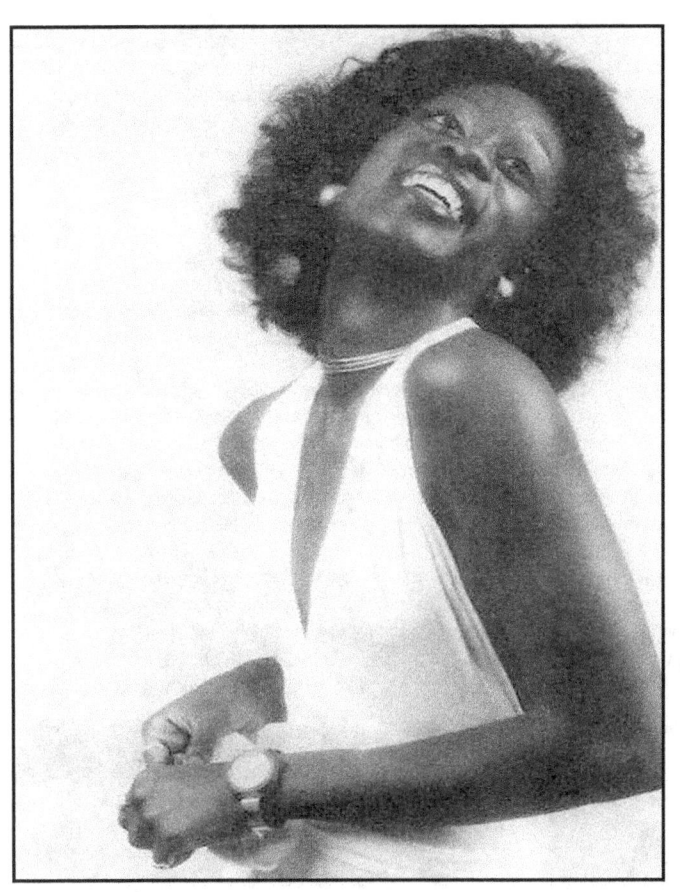

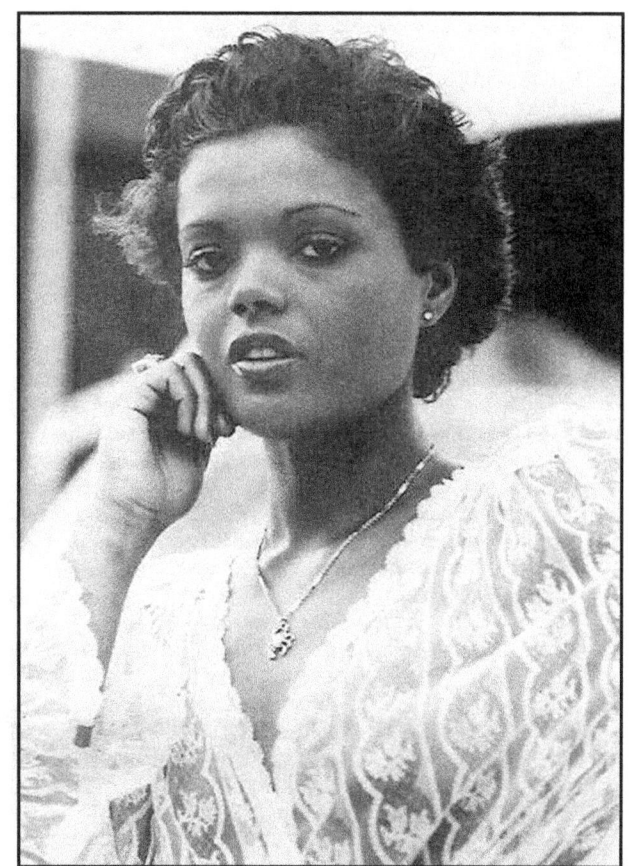

Model: Sheila Anderson

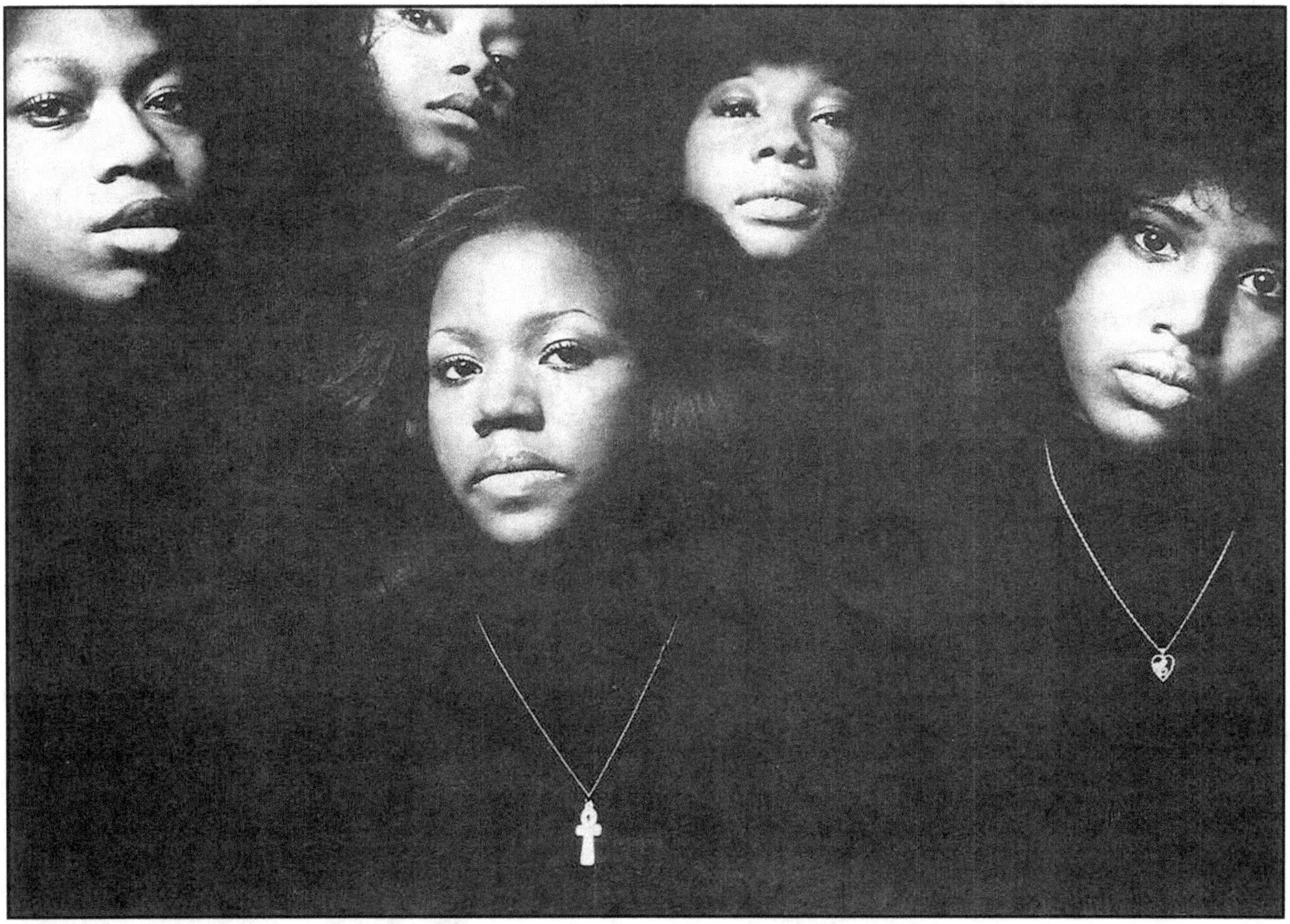

THE ETERNAL RHYTHMS OF

EARL 'FATHA' HINES

by Nikki Coleman

Having been blown around and nearly drowned in a Manhattan Monsoon, I must've looked like a drenched puppy or something as I greeted Earl "Fatha" Hines, if the expression on his face was any indication. I was no less shocked than he, because I was expecting to see an elderly-looking man (he was born on December 28, 1905). Yet a man who looked no more than 55 years old greeted me. As I set up the tape, I quickly scanned the hotel room. It was tiny, with a hint of bachelor clutter. Two things struck me especially....one was his exercise equipment, which explained why he was in such good physical shape, and his bags which were partially packed in readiness for a two-week, engagement in Nice, France the following day.

Fatha Hines is a truly modest man who has made a significant contribution in the development of jazz and, more specifically, the jazz piano. In fact, he's called "the Father of jazz piano." He is a contemporary of Louis Amstrong, Count Basie, and Duke Ellington, and has had his own band since 1928. Many questions flooded my mind as I sat and chatted with this living representative of Black musical history, and so I asked a few:

Impressions: Fatha Hines, what would you consider your most important contribution to the world of jazz?

F. Hines: Everybody has to have a start in music, and it's been my policy to help unknown artists and given them a start, and I think everybody who's in the position should do that -- reach down and help their own people. Like Charlie Parker, I needed a tenor sax player and he said, "I don't have a tenor, I have an alto," so I bought him a tenor. Ellington did the same thing. A lot of stars came out of his band -- Cootie Williams, Sonny Greer, Johnny Hodges.

So out of his deep humility, devotion to his art and his people, Fatha Hines sees helping young unknown Black artists as his most significant contribution to the world of jazz, and it's no small contribution, for it has enabled other Greats to be seen and heard. Yet according to Stanley Dance, a jazz critic from England who wrote Duke Ellington's autobiography and who is currently writing Fatha Hines' -- Fatha Hines is the Father of Bop. So I asked another qeustion that might give me a sense of his acknowledgement of his historical greatness:

Imp: What would you like people to

know about you?

F.H.: My profession is music and that's all I'm interested in. Everything I do in music is done because I love it, not for a bit of notoriety. Now, if they haven't seen or read what I've done--it's not for me to tell them. Anybody who's interested in me will come to see me or go to the libraries where they can read about me. I've left at least my fingerprints in the sands of time and my public has done that. They're the ones who've said I belong in the Hall of Fame.

Imp: Fatha Hines, do you know there are young Black people in their mid-20's who've never heard of you or someone like Dinah Washington because they're too busy keeping up with the latest rock group?

F.H.: Yes, that's true, but I fault the schools and the parents, especially of my race. The thing that I fault my race for is that they're so busy criticizing a man or woman who's made a bit of progress in this field, instead of giving respect to us because it's a tough field, especially for a Black person, and I'll tell you why. You see, there's all sorts of provisions made for the white artist. For instance, in the days of the big bands we couldn't play any of the big hotels, especially in the South. So the white big bands made more reputations for themselves than the Black bands, and they existed longer 'cause they had all those white hotels to play, a place to house them. When we did come out, it was because we did something the whites couldn't do. They could never imitate Ellington's sound or Basie's tempo--so they had to give credit where it was due. Now, instead of our race backing its own people to let the white race know how much they think of their own artist--they don't do it. We see it all the time in every city. They'll stay home and see you on the streets and talk about coming to see you, but they don't. The Jewish people--if Vic Damone is playing someplace, you can't get in for the Jews or Italians, or whatever he is. We envy each other too much, instead of getting behind our artist. You can't fault the youngsters too much, 'cause they don't know and nobody's telling them. The universities and high schools don't go into the history of Black music, either. But who digs all this stuff up and makes money off it--the white race. They realize what other countries think of the music from this country which was popularized by the Negro. Our mistake goes back to the family. I'm a race man and alway was, but today's parents don't really think of the child's future. For ins-

tance, when I tour Europe I see busloads of white Americans who're giving their kids a geographical education. We don't do that. We're too concerned about having a fur coat and two or three diamonds rings to go to places like that. The whites just wear ordinary clothes and sometimes their kids are barefoot. The same thing applies to my profession. I've argued time and time again--in order for you to have a voice, you've got to take part of an industry. Martin Luther King finally showed the world, by means of television, how important it is to vote. I've tried to tell people the importance of owning a part of the media, particularly television. Instead of standing on a street corner or in some bar talking about the latest car we bought or how much money we have, we ought to be trying to get a part of the television industry.

Imp: Speaking of industry, as a musician and artist you must have contact with the recording industry, which is notorious for exploiting Black artists. What are some of your firsthand accounts of this exploitation of Black artists?

F.H.: Over a period of years when they had T.O.B.A. (Theater Owners Booking Association), which was a Negro circuit because Negroes couldn't play the white circuit. These were small theaters and the owners were Jews who usually had a Black face up there to represent management, and most of the time, the Negroes who came to see these shows didn't even know that the owners were white.

Imp: Like the Apollo Theater?

F.H.: That's just what I'm talking about. So the Jews found out how whites went for the Negro musicians, comedians, and actors, and they soon got control of the theatrical world. The biggest mistake some Negros made (but they couldn't help themselves) was to let the Jews buy them. Here's a good example, one of the main writers for the Pittsburgh Courier used to go to the Apollo's Wednesday Amateur Hour (and he knew a lot about show business) and pick star material for this white organization. Right away the white organization would put him under contract. Now here's a young boy who's washing dishes somewhere making $15 or $20 a week and here comes a white man offering him a contract for 5 years at $100 a week. The white man knows what he's got, and he's a big man in two years, but he can't do a damn thing 'cause the white man's got him tied up. This is what's hampered the Negro, 'cause he has no organization to back him

up. I tried to open up a club two or three times in a spot where there was never a Negro businessman, in Jack London Square, Oakland, California. As soon as they found out there was a Negro owner with a white partner...they put the squeeze on my partner and I went around to all the Negro clubs to get $2,000, that's all I needed, but that's the way they squeezed me out.

Listen honey, I went broke in Chicago after I left the Grand Terrace. I left the Grand Terrace 'cause I couldn't stand that vise they put me in. You see, we Negros didn't realize that an agency works for you. You don't work for the agency. But the agency made Negros think they had to work for the agency and the agency would tell them, "you can't do this and you can't do that", and they would put them to work in any old kind of place--as long as they were getting their commission, that's all that mattered. That's why I'm out here by myself; I won't sign with any of them. I'm fortunate that I have a reputation and a lot of places want to book me, so I just let the agents fight over who gets the bookings. A lot of Negroes have gotten big and famous, but usually some finagling white man had them sewn up. And the conseqeunces are that they have no control over their lives and they have to walk away from the people that mean a lot to them. That's a heck of a darn thing, to have to give yourself away, if you're an artist. I have a girl (Marva Josie) who's been singing with me for 8 years and everywhere we go she stops a house and nobody can point a finger at her. If she gets up there she'll be the only Black gal I know who got up there without some strings attached. You see what I'm talking about? This is what I'm fighting all by myself. I've gone to recording companies to talk about recording her, but without success. If I were a white man it would be different. Now if I turn her loose and she goes to some recording company and spends a night or a vacation with some of them? Yeah, she'll get some recording dates tomorrow. But she says she doesn't want to do that. She'd rather stay with my organization, even if she never gets a record, than give herself away like that. And I appreciate her for that. We artists have been subjected to a lot of things, Nikki, you'd just be surprised. I usually just keep my mouth shut. For instance, talent often failed to show for the Johnny Carson show and a little Black trumpet player by the name of Clark Terry would time and time again fill in for these people. Yet when Johnny Carson needed a band director, who did they pick but the man who was sitting next to Clark Terry and stealing everything he could from him. So this white man was making all the money when Clark really should have had the job. But Clark Terry had no organization. Who could say anything to C.B.S. or N.B.C.?

Imp: That's pretty typical of the relationship between Black musicians and white ones, or just simply white men and Black men. Each decade has had its white group who stole from Black musicians and reaped all the rewards, including being able to leave fortunes to their children. What I really want to know is, have you personally been ripped off by the people who control the entertainment industry?

F.H.: Well, I was with the Frazier Agency, who came to California to get me to work with Louis Armstrong, and I had worked with him before when we were young, so I wanted to work with him again. And I did for three years. Well, my contract ran out. I had a contract with Frazier himself with 75% publicity. So I told them Louis and I shouldn't have to fool with a band anymore, night after night. We should have our own act -- Louis was big enough to do that. Well, they didn't like my idea and Louis didn't have anyone to support him. I was ready to quit after my two weeks' notice--Joe Frazier, himself, made it so that if I didn't work as a sideman with Louis, I would be blackballed for two years. Well, my original contract had not been with Louis but with the agency, plus we were all band leaders who worked with Louis, Jack Teagarden and all of us, not sidemen. I refused to work as a sideman and I refused to sign with Louis (if things didn't work out this time, I could pick up my own band again because I had signed with the agency). So you see, that's just another example of how easy it is to be abused in this industry.

Fatha Hines was born in Duquesne, Pa., 1905 (Capricorn) and he grew up in Pittsburg, and it's no wonder that he places so much responsibility on Black parents. His father was his idol. He always wanted to have his own band like his dad who played coronet and led his own brass band. He tried playing coronet for a while but it hurt his ears, so he stopped that instrument and fooled around with a few more. Finally, his mother, who is an organist, saw him imitating her at the organ one day and decided that he should start playing the piano. She traded in her organ for a piano

and piano lessons for Earl. He went on to study music in high school and college. Although he was not able to finish his college education, he got what he thought he needed. Surprisingly, he wanted to be a classical or concert pianist, but he was told that he'd be 90 years old before anybody would recognize him, here in this country. So his sights had changed before he left college, and (surpirse number two) he left college because he was so popular that he was unable to attend his classes.

Eileen Southern, in The Music of Black Americans, *says that, "Hines developed a piano style in which his right hand played melodic figures similar to those of a trumpet, but in octaves, while his left hand provided the firm bass of an orchestral rhythm section. Hines' so-called 'trumpet piano' style was widely imitated by other pianists, Black and white, of the period."*

Stanley Dance said that Hines did away with the importance of the left hand of "Stride Piano," which was an offshoot of ragtime. In the 20's and 30's he was the Chicago extension of Harlem pianists, and it was there at the Grand Terrace Ballroom that he earned distinction as an orchestra leader.

During my interview with Fatha Hines, Stanley Dance, the jazz critic, came to pay him a visit, and as Mr. Dance and I talked, Fatha Hines dozed off to sleep. Mr. Dance must have read my thoughts for he immediately informed me that Fatha had played a concert in Delaware on Sunday and had driven back to N.Y. early Monday morning and was undoubtedly quite tired from the trip. "Amazing," I said, whereupon Fatha Hines awoke and I proceeded to wind up my interview:

Imp: Fatha, have you been or are you married?

F.H.: Yes, I'm still married with two daughters, one of whom is Ginea Hines who played the babysitter on Diahann Carrol's T.V. show JULIA. My family and I have our permanent residence on the West Coast.

Imp: Fatha, who would you say of the young serious musicians you have influenced?

F.H.: Well, I've had a lot of them come around but they've never said that I influenced them. They never tell me. I only know by what they tell other people.

Imp: Does that mean that you only communicate with your own contemporaries? Don't you ever talk with young serious jazz artists like McCoy Tyner or Doug Carne?

F.H.: I never see them. They don't come around me, and my own contemporaries are thinning out. I've tried to get the unions to take the restrictions off jam sessions so these young musicians could come on the floor and communicate together, and so we could all get to know each other. But I haven't been successful, so I don't know the young musicians that you're speaking of.

Imp: Who were some of the now famous musicians who played with you?

F.H.: Teddy Wilson, Nat Cole, Stan Kenton, just to mention a few.

Imp: Traditionally, Black musicians have had to play dives, honky-tonks and whore houses to survive. Were you also forced to play those kinds of places?

F.H.: Sure, in Pittsburgh. They didn't call them honky-tonks, but I've played in houses of prostitution because I was too young to play anywhere else, and the only time the white man came by there, was 'cause they heard they had a young black boy on piano who could really play.

Imp: I hear a few of the younger musicians say rather glibly that when things start getting rough, they have to go out and find a patron of the arts. What they're referring is a white women who will give them money and/or position and who will be their woman at the same time. Is this tradition among Black musicians?

F.H.: That goes back to the old tradition that the only free people in this country are the white man and the Black woman. Most of them go for the musician out of curiosity because they've been forbidden to know each other as children growing up. Many white men think that sex is best with a Black woman and white women believe that sex is best with a Black man. Now there's a certain amount of "prestige" connected with having a new car and a white girl as far as musicians go. Most of the time these gals were considered outcasts by their own people and the only people who would have her were the folks in Harlem. She could be a lot freer up there in Harlem, and most other men had to work in offices or daytime jobs, but the musician had a lot of time to play if she wanted to play.

Imp: What is music's relationship to our culture? Does it reflect our culture or predict for the future or what?

F.H.: I don't know what you mean. Do you mean is there a future for what's happening now in music? The musician of today doesn't really love what he's doing. It's a commercial thing now and all they want is a new house or a new car or...

Imp: Wait just a minute, that's the rock star. There are young serious jazz musicians around who have a much harder time than rock stars.

S. Dance: Well, even that's questionable. For every rock star who makes it, there are thousands who don't make it.

Imp: Sure, but Earth, Wind and Fire has a larger mass appeal than McCoy Tyner.

S.D.: Because he's almost too intellectual for the average person.

F.H.: During the swing era we played things the people could understand. But they got away from that and started playing all sorts of tempos and pretty soon the musician started playing for the musician, than for the public. When rock came in, it was something the people hadn't heard in a long time and it gave them a chance to pat their foot again. I like the idea of rock--but improve on it and try to find out how

much farther you can make it go instead of just trying to make it a commercial thing to buy as many cars as you can with it.

It was getting late and Fatha Hines dozed off once again. I wondered if he was tired from more than his trip to Delaware, and if he would really prefer being at home with his wife instead of going to France, Australia, and God knows where. I know that white musicians of his stature and age range don't have to keep such a hectic schedule. They've made enough money off Black music not to have to keep that pace any longer, while the originators must work at music or something else. Of course, Stanley Dance, in a manner that is typically omniscient and forever English said:

"Oh no, he loves what he's doing. In 1954 he was going to quit music and open a store and I persuaded him to come here and play the Little Theater Concerts. He came and started a new

career. He only plays two- and three-week engagements now. He seldom does one-nighters, like the one in Delaware, anymore."

Mr. Dance and I talked a while longer and I discovered that he has a nostalgia for the jazz of the 20's and 30's. I have no doubts that Fatha Hines loves what he's doing, but it is hard work and he could certainly reach a much larger audience and possibly make as much money by simply doing a half-dozen guest appearances on T.V. a year. Perhaps then he could spend time filling the communications or generation gap that seems to exist between our older artists and our younger ones. As to the future of jazz, Mr. Dance gives a very poor prognosis. Jazz is only 50 years old and he feels that it won't be around for another 50. What does that say about us, since we are jazz? ✿

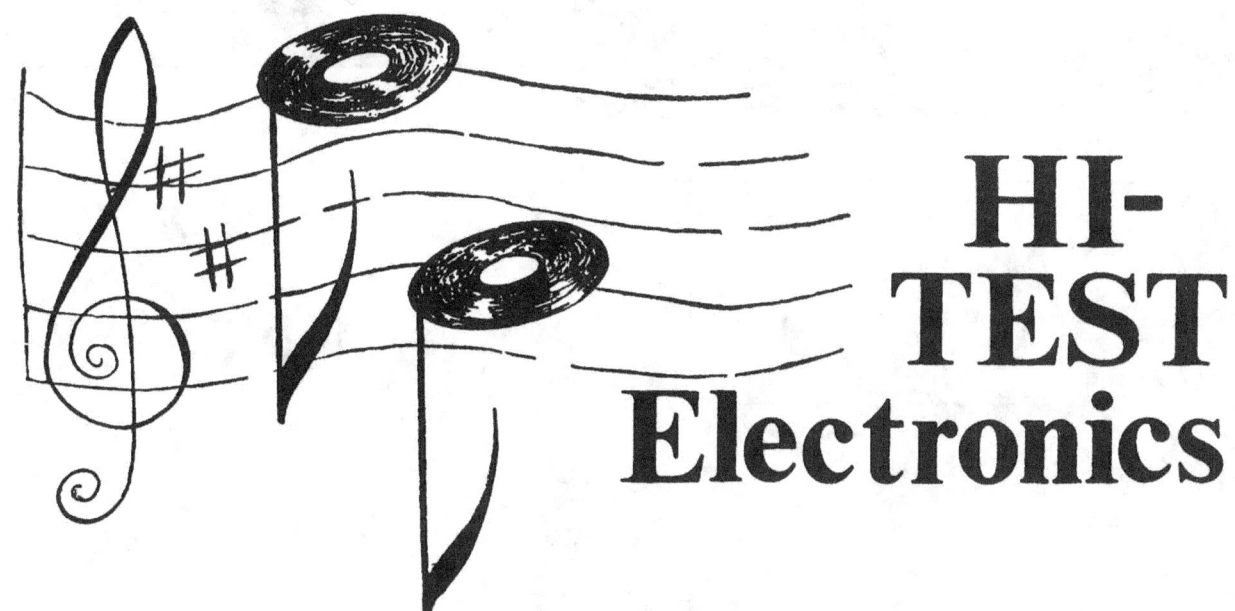

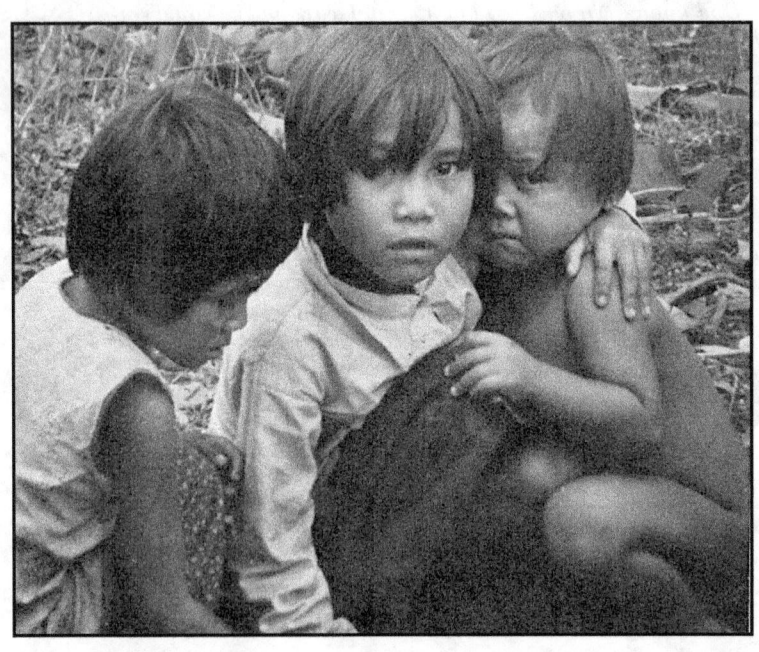

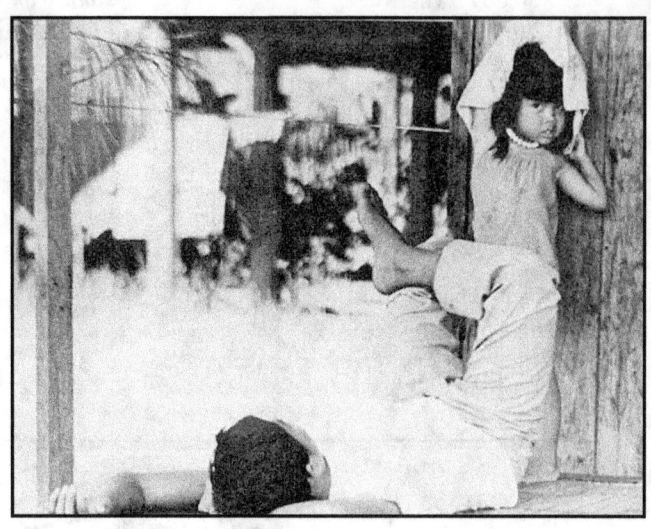

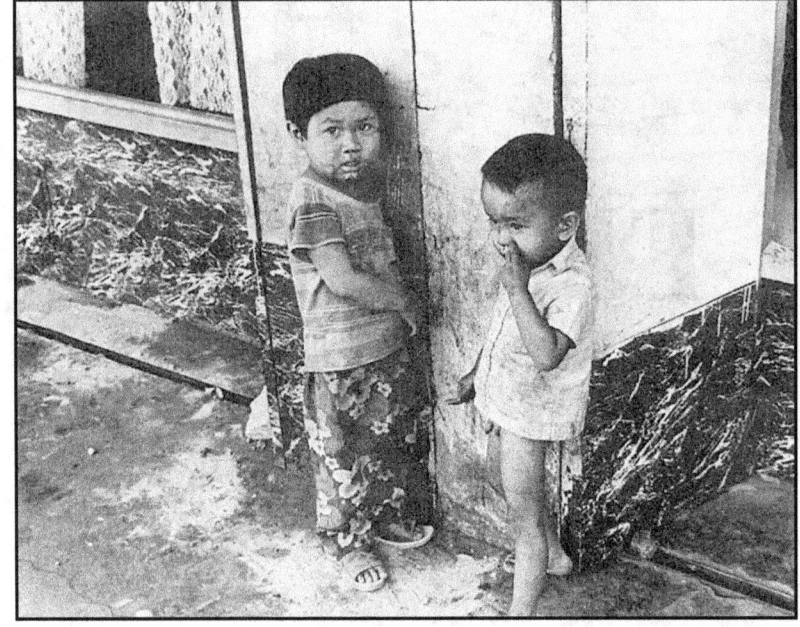

IN A
CHILD'S EYE

by bob bryan

(Thailand '71)

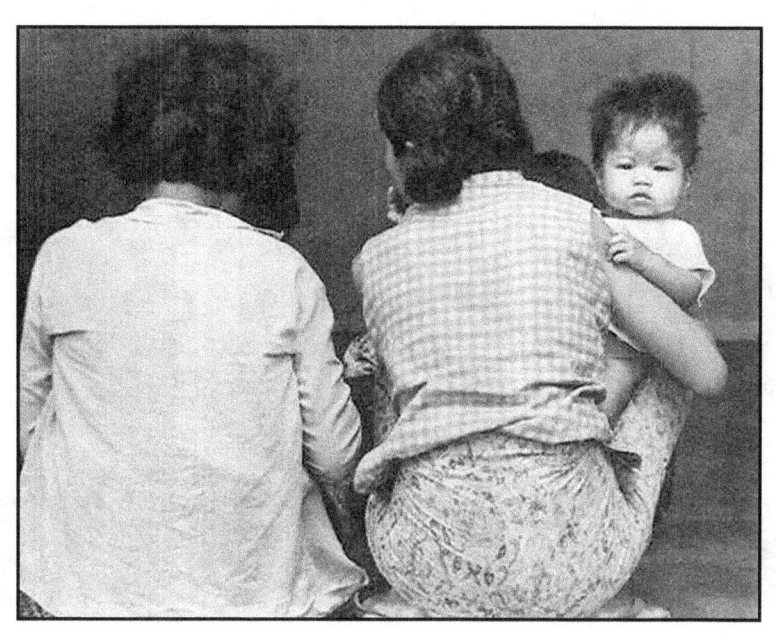

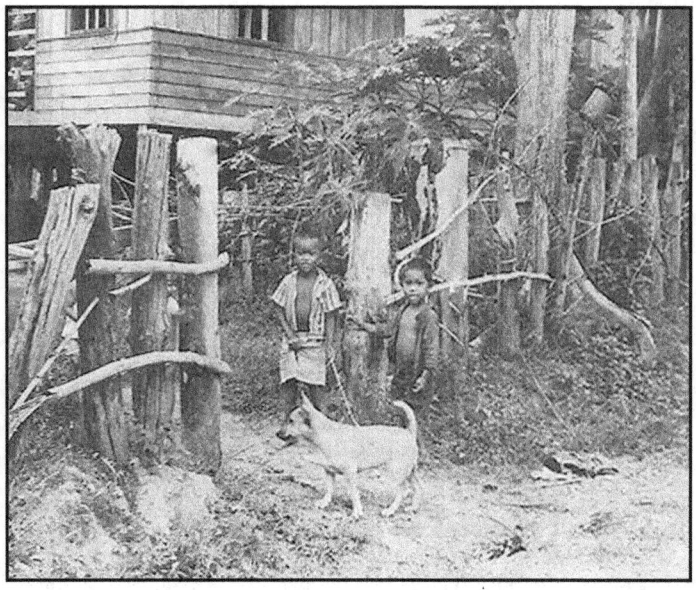

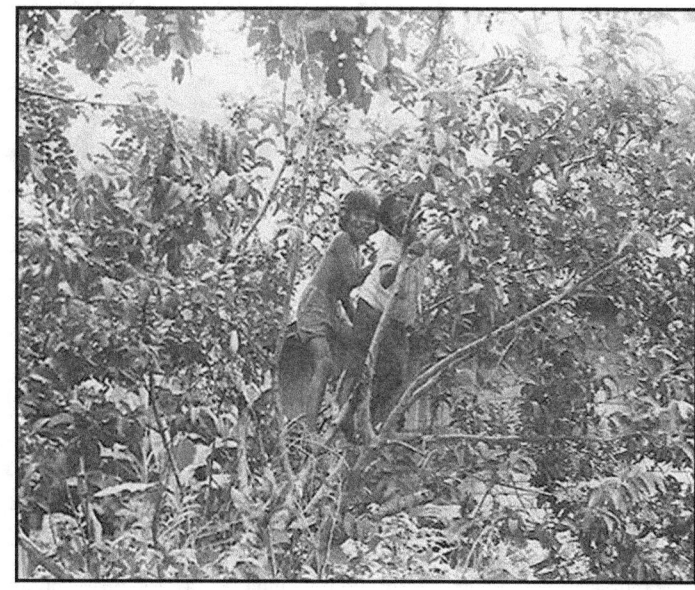

Oh, natty, natty,

Natty 21,000 miles away from home

Oh, natty, natty,

And that's a long way

for natty to be from home...

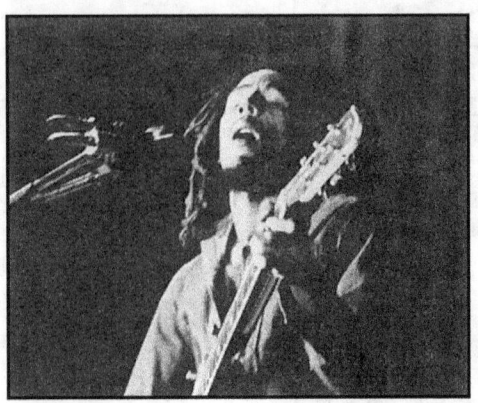 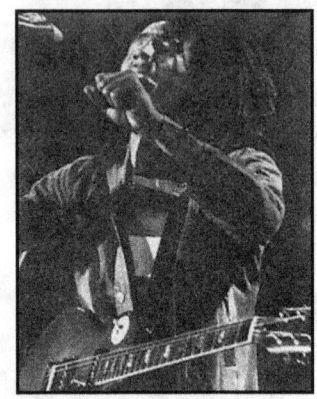 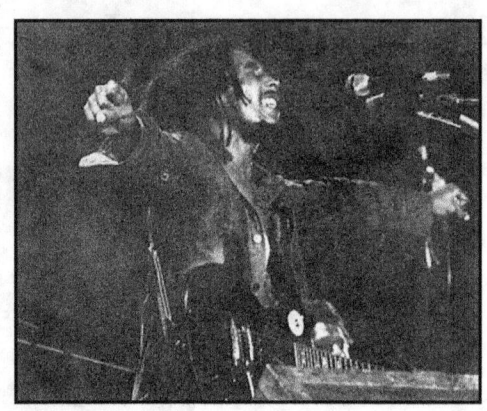

"... you got to love yourself
before you can love Reggae."

BOB MARLEY

by Bob Bryan
edited by Michael Hyatt and Yvonne Moran

Impressions: With your music, are you trying to teach or educate people? Is that what you're trying to do with the music?

B. Marley: Well, the music is the music. No music do plenty t'ings, 'cause you can't control the music. The music is really to contact people and because these are the last days.... It's gonna get more wicked, you know. It's going to get to the extreme wickedness 'till it start to run over. I mean it's running over now, but you still got to have more than that, because many more will have to die.... So the music come out of the music. The people who know the music is people like me and you — *the living man* — you know, *God.* Reggae's like acceptance, you know. You've got to be proud...you've got to love yourself before you can love Reggae.

Imp: Reggae here in this country has by and large not been given the play that it should have, as compared to other kinds of music. Why do think that is so?

B.M.: Well again, you know, it's a dangerous game hunting a radio station. You have thousands of record releases every year. Now, you have people way up — guys who don't know — who, if them don't like your record, them push it in a corner...all them t'ings 'appen. You have plenty records that go on the charts and some that don't go that far. A guy who gets the most promotion, he can win. It's not that people are dealing with justice. People not dealing with nothing, you know. People are just dealing with the way them think other people might think; that's how people will deal with it, you know what I mean. A guy feels that if he doesn't like it, well...nobody else won't like it.

But over the years Reggae music wasn't up to standard to compete. Like, you can't put it with other music and compare it. Owing to the fact that the musicians been ripped off and a lot of t'ings 'appen to the people

who play the music...the guy who owns the studio, he becomes the artist, the musician and that's it for that Reggae record. So you find that with Reggae music, no one was really *dealing* with it. Only we deal with it the right way.

Imp: There's a large Jamaican community here, yet it still isn't pushed...

B.M.: No, but where the Jamaicans are you have Jamaican record shops, you know. In Jamaica we do not own our recordings. You have a guy who buys the record and bring it to a record company. Well, this guy has a pressin' plant downstairs. Him get your record and...he's got a stamp press....and him press the record down there and sell them on the black market. Records are a funny t'ing. When the record is ready, if people come to your shop to buy it and you don't have it they tend to forget about it after that.

Imp: So distribution is very important?

B.M.: Yeah. So the distribution

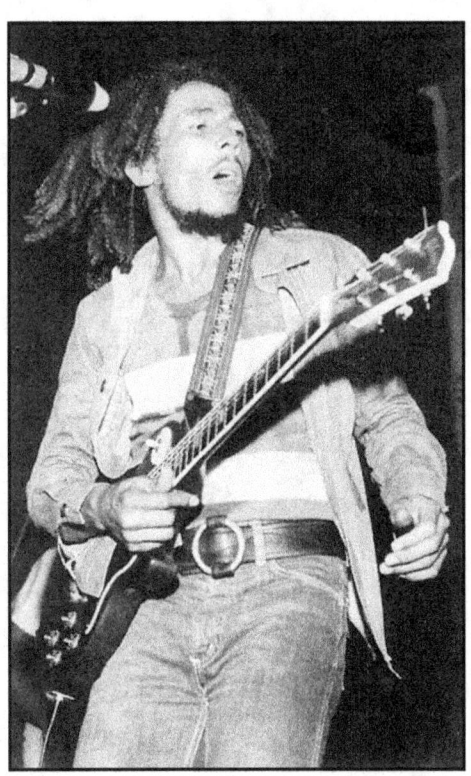

Photo by Harold H. Belgrave
a Caribbeat Production Photo

English guy; India belongs to the Indian...you understand. Africa belongs to the Black man. The Black man suffer many t'ings through white man. You know, like slavery and all them t'ings, but it comes from the Black man because the Black man don't want to know God. The Black man don't want to know God...that's why him always suffer. The Black man don't care to know that he is the ruler for the earth and he should live like the ruler of the earth instead of living like someone who gave up his post. Black man really give up him post, you know, and that's why so many t'ings are happening to us all over the the earth. None of us care for Ethiopia; none of us love Africa. We talk of Africa but we don't love Africa. That is what happen; that is why it's so important for the Black man to realize that Africa is ours. You can't have America. You can't have stock in Africa, you know what I mean; you've got to *own* it. Leave here and go there and help the people, then come back here again if you want to. You can't make it *part* of your life because that's what the *whole* thing is about. That is our foundation, that's our roots. We don't have any roots here and we're just strung about. We are the REAL PEOPLE! The people who dem take from *the place.* So we

ble...when it reach out they will know that His Imperial Majesty of Ethiopia is the Conqueror of the Land of Judah. The Bible was written thousands of years before the "revelation." When the Bible reveals itself it will show that, yes, Moses was black, you know. You don't to have to know plenty things. Moses was black! Solomon was black! Jeremiah was black! All the people in the Bible were black, you know!

Imp: In your new album, NATTY DREAD, there's one cut called *Revolution*. What kind of revolution are you talking about?

B.M.: Well...it's a trickyfied revolution. Like a Rastafarian revolution. In that, you see the scientists and them guys will go as far as to tell you that....the atmosphere cuts and meets the air and causes noise we call thunder. That is not so. Our God is a thundering God, in lightning! Maybe it's the atmosphere that makes it do that, but you have a Power behind it that causes the atmosphere to do that...which is a Man. Which is I and I and I and I. But God cannot be God without the people and yet he is God without anyone. Now, our God is *the* God...the right God, the God that created the earth. But it's like Black man don't want to see it.

---

wasn't...dem didn't really ever have distribution. A guy only try to press 500 and sell it off because he knows that he is doing something illegal. Only sometimes, if him find him can sell like 10,000...him go ahead and do it.

Imp: Well, what is the political reality in Jamaica for black people?

B.M.: The political reality for Black people in Jamaica is that Black people don't really know them position in politics in Jamaica. Jamaican people bright, you know, and dumb. But you got more dumb than bright in politics. You have plenty people who vote and don't know who they vote for. That's how politics goes! A politician will say, "Well, the farmers will be getting $19 this year," and you hear a thousand people say, "Hooray." Madness!

Imp: ...I get on the subways and I see all these people sitting or standing there with these newspapers...they're all reading the same newspapers...

B.M.: Yeah!

Imp: The same messages are coming out at you...

B.M.: Forceful...they're not doing it freely. It's just...

Imp: Impact, it's pushed at you.

B.M.: Yeah. You have to deal with that as a trend. You know, you have to feel like you have some input.

Imp: Like you're part of it.

B.M.: And them is only idiots, fools. And them are the people that other people think are the real people.

Imp: What are the Rastafarians?

B.M.: Well, a Rasta man is a man who knows that Ethiopia is Zion...that's the heaven that people talk of. Like, me personally don't know everyt'ing about certain. t'ings. I know that England belongs to the

> ".... a Rasta man is a man who knows that Ethiopia is Zion...."

couldn't expect it to be like New York or...yet you have places worse than New York. People should realize that we are the head, that we are the wisest people on the earth.

Imp: There has certainly been a systematic brainwashing job applied...convincing Blacks that they are nothing.

B.M.: That is the thing. It is not only that, but it's Black convincing Black, you know. In the beginning the earth was black, you understand. The first man put on the earth was black, can you dig it...good! I mean man...but it can't be a prejudice thing again.

Imp: ...or we'd be making the same mistake that they made?

B.M.: ...can't make it a prejudice thing and then you can't give yourself away either. You have to just live. But you got to know where you want to live.

Imp: Bob, what is your goal?

B.M.: My goal is Ethiopia. But certain cycles happenin' in the meantime. Me, personally, don't come from here (America) and go to Ethiopia, but when I go to Ethiopia...like thousands of people from America have to be going too. That is the thing right now. Because this is the Bible (reaching over to his desk)...plenty man turn down the Bible...plenty man don't want to read the Bible. Him say white man wrote the Bible and blah, blah, blah. But God said he shall put it into their hearts to write, you know that means the interpretation of the Bi-

Imp: Why is it that Black people don't want to see it?

B.M.: Because they're not ready. You see, it's the Black people who need to see, you know. In my records I talk about the people who've gone astray...I talk about people who've gone astray that have babies. It's them babies that we have to steer. We can't bring them up in places like New York to stumble up and down that kind of way...never

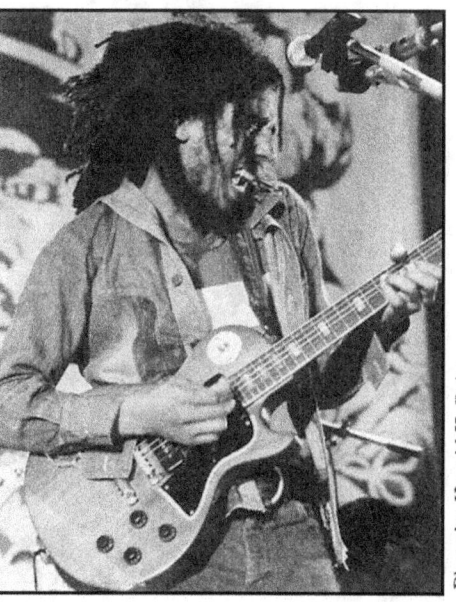

Photo by Harold H. Belgrave

Cont'd on page 49

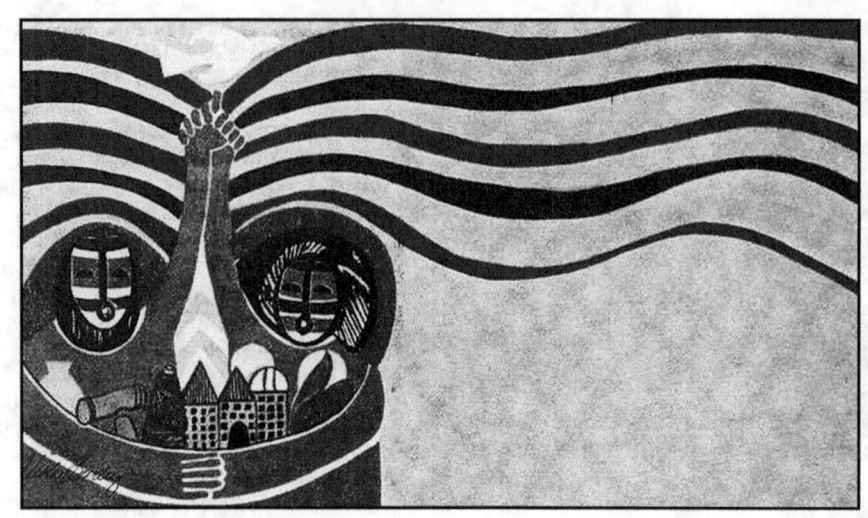

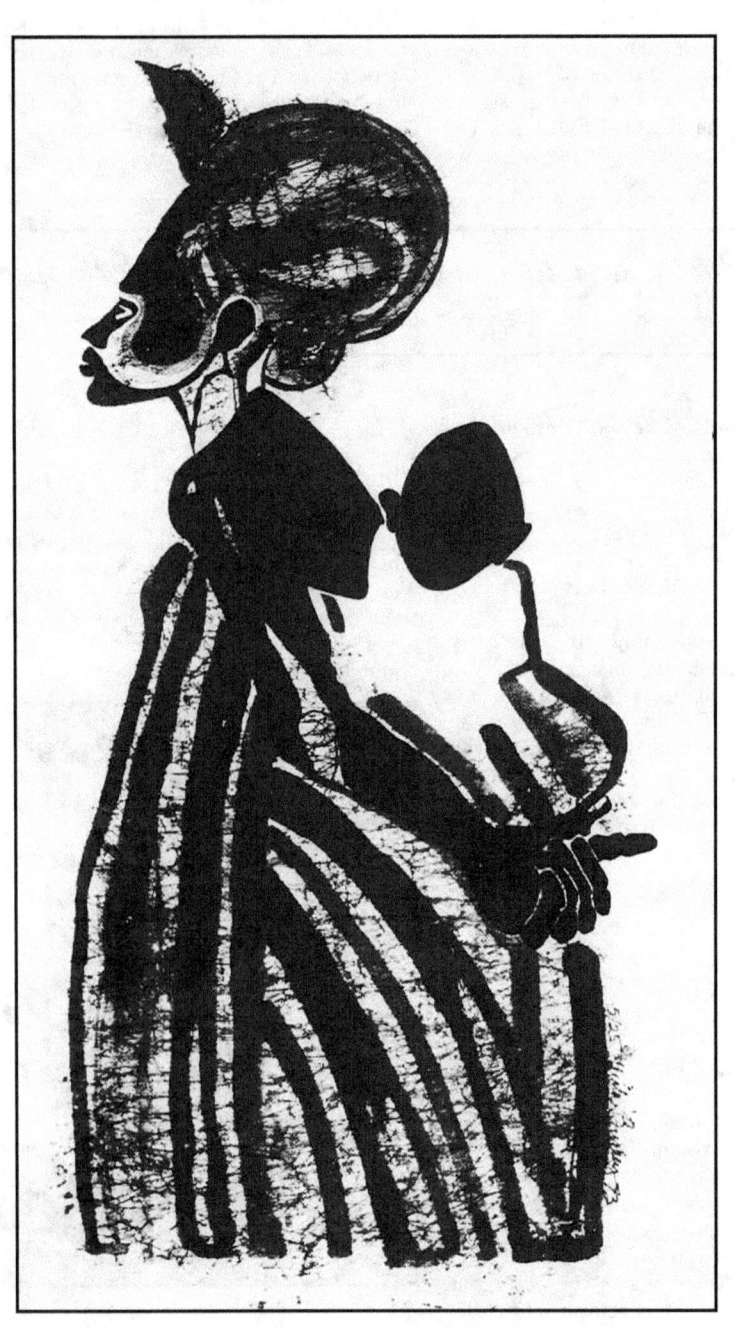

Viola Burley

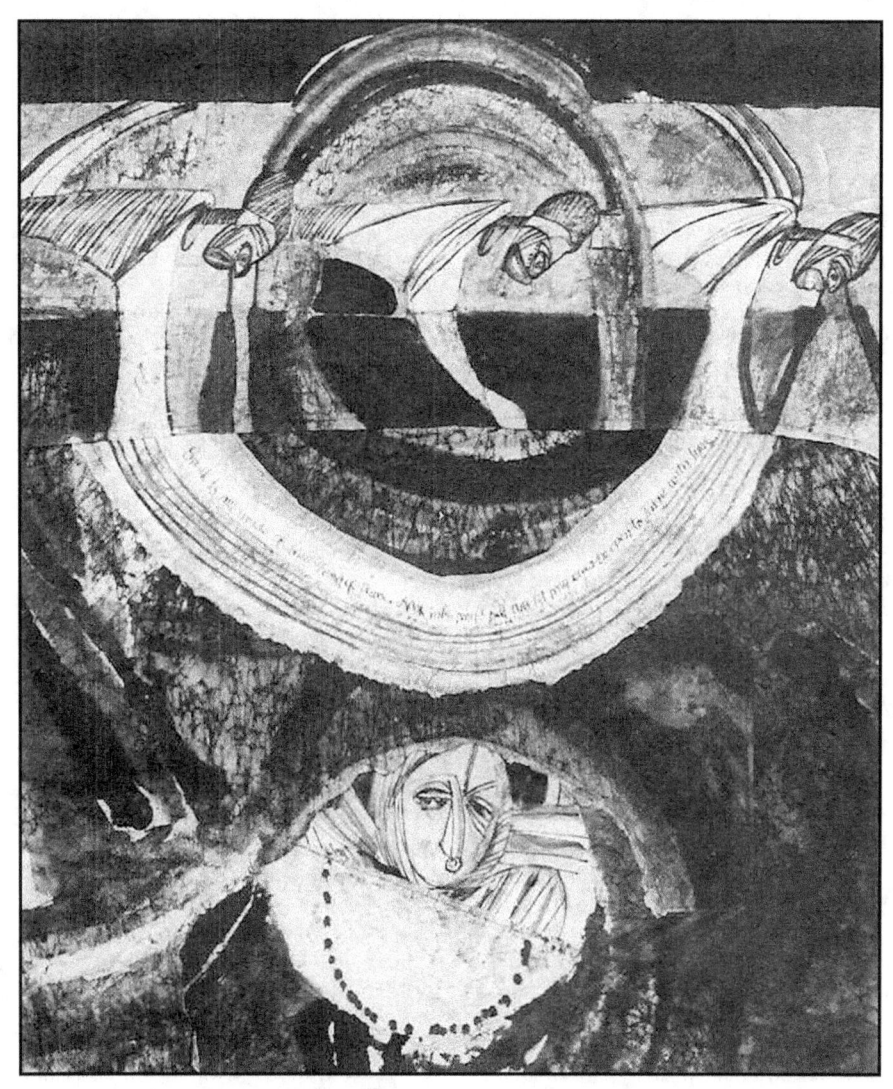

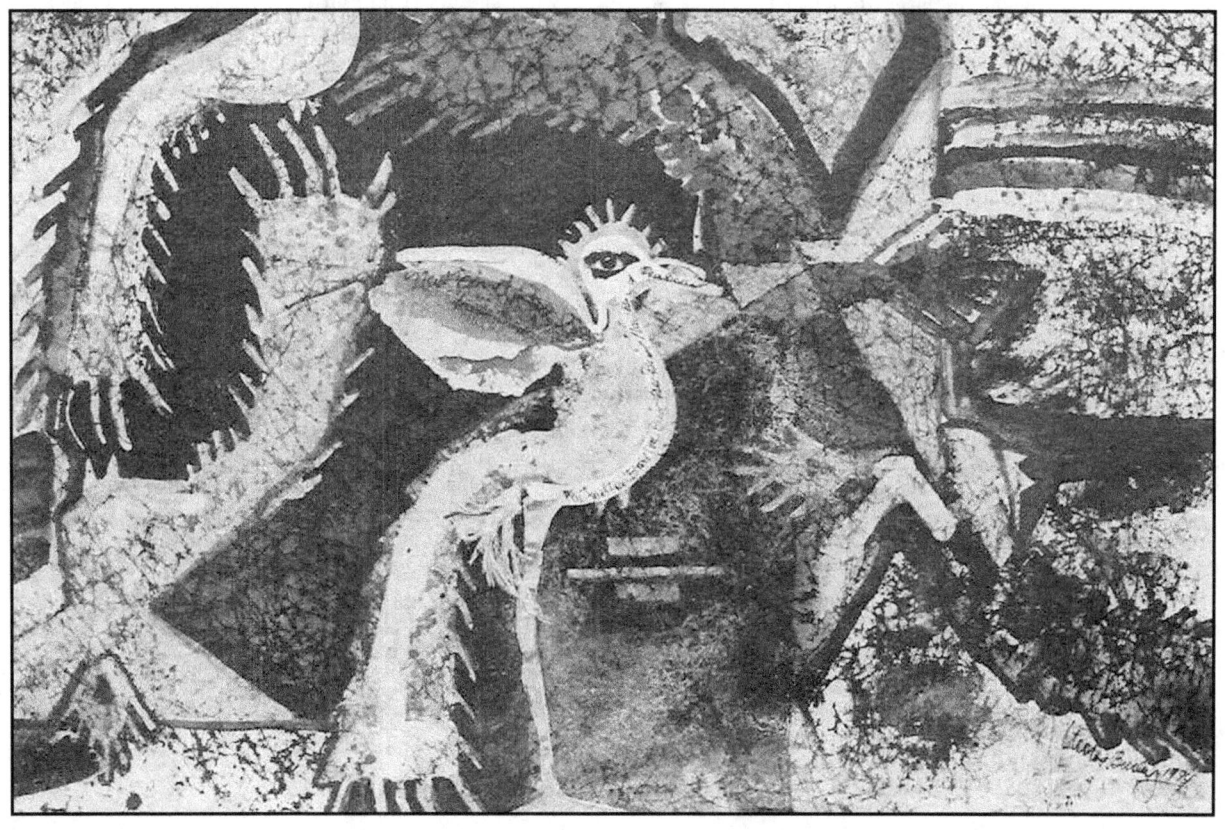

THE CONFRONTATION

In considering the question of the Black image in the media and its effect upon Black people, another question came to mind: the responsibility of the Black artist for the images that he creates.

One day recently I discussed these issues with Martie Charles, a playwright who was one of the many talented artists involved with the New Lafayette Theater. I asked her to write an essay based upon the points that came up in our discussion.

— Calvin Wilson

by MARTIE CHARLES

Dear Calvin:

After giving much thought to an article for your very fine magazine on Black Arts and Culture, I've decided to deal with the writer's accountability by relating an incident that occurred at the Schomberg Library.

It actually happened on a hot June morning of this year, in the memorabilia-filled research room of the Schomberg. Seated at one of those long and familiar wooden work tables seen so often in the library, I waited for the librarian to return with my books. My pocketbook, a few sharpened pencils and a canary legal pad, on top of which lay a stack of index cards, which were on the table. Restless, I picked up the cards, which contained information that I had gathered from the files the previous morning, and began to thumb through them, putting into one pile those that she was locating and in another those that I would read next. Anxious to begin my work of developing a dramatization for a lucheon to be given in honor of the Honorable Wallace D. Muhammad's visit to New York, I finished arranging the cards and began to write a tentative outline. My aim was to write a script based on the thoughts of the Black woman of America from the time she stepped upon these shores on to today; and after hearing the Supreme Minister's enlightening teaching on woman and on the impact of the Eve, Delilah and Jezebel images upon woman's self-concept and the resulting behavior that these images generate, my work took on an even greater meaning. So often the Black woman is labeled as the one female on earth who is available to any and every man on the planet. Whenever we look for ourselves in the literature, it is the concept of the "free woman" that is put before us, and so it was my hope to locate the work of those who understood what was happening and did not yield mentally to the oppressive conditions in which they found themselves, but who cried out thru their writings against injustice, and whose beings fought the images that were forced upon them. I wanted to structure a work that would highlight such thoughts chronologically, thus revealing to the audience the development of the mind in its ability to articulate to a greater and greater degree what was happening to us as a people, with emphasis on the woman.

Looking up from my writing, I saw the librarian approaching, and, as I reached eagerly for the books, she explained that several of the periodicals were unavailable. I thanked her, wait-ing for her to give me the books.

"You're welcome," she returned, and, after some hesitation, asked, "Are you Martie Charles?"

I indicated that I was, remembering that I had signed the slips as Martha Evans-Charles. Her eyes brightened and a slight smile appeared on her face as she sat in the chair next to me, resting the books on her lap.

"Did you write the play **Jamimma**?" she went on.

"Yes I did," I responded.

"Tell me," she asked sincerely, "why did Jamimma take all of what she did from him?" Assuming "him" to mean Omar, I asked, "What do you think?"

Sitting back, she responded, "Well, I hope it wasn't for love, because...she paused and a quizzical look came into her face. "Was it for love?" she queried. "I can't see what kind of love that was."

"It depends on your understanding of love," I answered.

That annoyed her. "Couldn't she see what was goin' on?" she pursued, her voice rising at the end of the question.

"Well," I replied, "no, she could not see. When we are blind, we are blind to something definite. We are not just abstractly blind." Her head tilted, and the quizzical look reappeared as I continued: "When we are blind, we are unable to discern something either physically or mentally. A person may be blind to light, and to the physical objects that light reveals; however, that very same person, after listening to a conversation, can tell you exactly where the speaker is coming from." She smiled, indicating understanding, and I went on. "That person is not blind to human behavior and the meaning that lies behind it. There are those of us who see very well with the physical eye, but who are without the mental ability to interpret what we see, thereby protecting ourselves. This was Jamimma's problem, and you must understand something of her self-concept in order to further understand the things that she allowed to happen to her."

"She must not have thought much of herself," she injected, and before I could answer, she cameback with, "But do you think that Black women are still like that?"

"Like what," I asked, hoping to get a clearer picture of Jamimma's impact upon her.

"Taking anything from a man!" she shot back. "Don't you think she's more independent?"

"Depends on what we as women consider important," I responded. "Was Jamimma a real person?" she questioned with penetrating eyes. I smiled, having been asked this so many times before. "No, not really," I answered. "She is an attitude, a conglomeration of women, a pattern of behavior." Then I asked, "Tell me, would you say that Jamimma respected herself?"

I received a blunt "no" for an answer.

I continued. "Would you say that self-respect is what bothered you about Jamimma?"

"Yes," she responded, without any hesitation.

"Well, then," I continued, "you take that same searchlight of things that we allow to happen to us because of the importance that we attach to something, and you will find Jamimma, or the spirit of Jamimma, in some very interesting places. Many of us consider a job important, and so we take stuff that another person couldn't possibly deal with. We become blind to the behavior of that which we desire to embrace, if seeing the truth of that thing gets in the way of our having it."

"Yes, we allow things to happen to us," she agreed with an accompanying nod.

"That's right," I continued, "and we have difficulty with anyone who tries to show us the object of our desire as it is. That is why Jamimma argued with her sister. What you don't know can't hurt you, right? Wrong! Ignorance deprives us of the ability and the freedom to see. We see after we know. The more we know about something, the better we can make a judgement about it. Jamimma wanted a home, a husband and child. She wanted fulfillment as a woman, and she settled for these things on the level that Omar offered them to her. But had she possessed a greater knowledge about herself, and a better understanding of the concept of woman and of being true to yourself and your human dignity before you can be true to anyone else, she would have done a better job of solving her problem."

She replied after a period of silence. "Well, why did you let it end that way? I mean, it was very powerful and all, but how did she know that in a few years he wouldn't do the same thing as Omar?"

"Interestingly enough," I answered, "my greatest problem with Jamimma was how to end it. I know that the solution of her problem was knowledge. Had Jamimma been given greater knowledge, she would have been able to grow from where she was to another level. With growth would have come understanding of Omar and where he was in life in relation to where she was, as well as a solution to her problem."

We sat silently for a while, her head moving back and forth. She smiled and thanked me for talking with her, and I thanked her for her questions. Putting the books on the table, she stood up, and as she slid the chair back into place, she told me that she had been an actress who was now enrolled in college studying for a degree in medicine.

It's interesting that this should happen to me as I was about to embark upon another project that meant so much to me, as all of my works do. As she walked away, I began to reflect on what had just taken place, and how it "brought home" the responsibility of the artist for the images that we put forth. We handle ideas and images. The people who hear or see our work very often take these ideas and images in and act upon them, which speaks of an awesome responsibility resting upon the shoulders of the writer. Too often, too many writers refer to their work in drama or film as pure entertainment and nothing more, but in the face of the sophisticated mind-manipulation that is going on today, such a statement is childishly naive.

The day of accountability is fast approaching, if not already here, and we, who have suffered under some of the worst images that movieland could find to represent us, should welcome such a day. We should encourage our people to question us. They should know the motive behind a work, and if for any reason the work is not clear in what it is saying, or if it crosses up the mind, brings frowns and looks of misunderstanding, then the audience has a right to straighten things out by checking with the mind that put the work out there. I believe that questioning is a part of the thinking process, and as a people we've never been encouraged to question. We were raised under the "hush your mouth" kind of mentality; the very atmosphere discouraged our questioning. Consequently, our growth has been very slow; but this is a new day, and we should be about progress and movement into a better life, upliftment, enlightenment, new levels of understanding, pulling our people up, and pulling ourselves up. We should be about the exchange of ideas, questions and answers, clarity, truth and love thru knowledge.✿

Martha Evans-Charles is a playwright, poet, and assistant Professor of Speech and Drama for the City University of New York at Medgar Evers College. She is scheduled to have a reading of her new play Asante *on October 13th at the Black Theatre Alliance's Frank Silvera Playwright's Workshop under the direction of Garland Thompson. Her plays, in addition to* Jamimma *and* Asante *, are the following:* Where We At; Job Security; Black Cycle; *and* American Blacks Are Very Strange *(in progress).*

For information regarding her plays she may be contacted at:
Medgar Evers College, Humanities Division
The City University of New York
1150 Carroll Street
Brooklyn, New York 11225

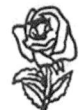

ed bullins

is the winner of this year's New York Drama Critics Circle Award for his play, "The Taking of Miss Janie." After an initial run at the New Federal Theater, the play was moved to Lincoln Center. This interview was held at the Public Theater, where Mr. Bullins is conducting a playwrights' workshop.

by Calvin Wilson

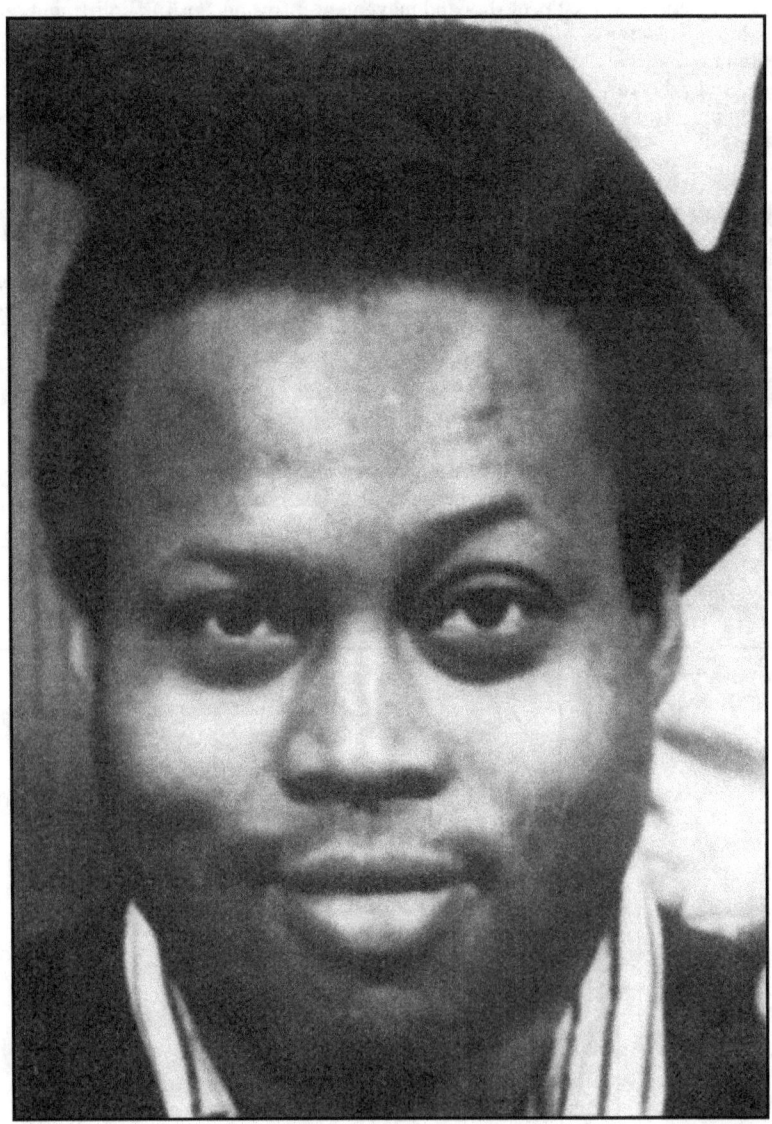

Impressions: You've been a playwright for many years now. Has your style of writing changed?

Bullins: Well, I don't know. If you compared some of my early plays to my older plays I don't know what the changes would be anymore.

Imp: How do you go about teaching a person to write plays?

Bullins: You can't teach anybody to write plays. You can show them some of the things that they can do, suggest some things, coach. You can try to stimulate them and argue with them. But you can't teach something like that. It's dependent upon the person's creativity, their facility with the language, the written language, the spoken language, their ability to visualize things on the stage and put them on paper and make it dramatic. It takes a lot of things, it has to come out of you.

Imp: What does this "coaching" involve?

Bullins: They have to write, first. They can't just come in like a clean sheet of paper. They have to be trying to write something, and then I can help them make it better, perhaps. Try to squeeze more out of them, if they're willing.

Imp: Do you see your role at the Public Theater as being similar to the position you held at the New Lafayette Theater?

Bullins: Well, I've just been here at the Public Theater a matter of weeks, and so I guess my role hasn't been that defined. The New

Lafayette Theater was some time ago, and I keep in touch with the organization in some ways, so I imagine they would complement one another and be dissimilar in some ways.

Imp: How important do you feel it is for Black theater to be located in the community, where the people will have the easiest access to it? Do you feel that the Black theater audience is now more willing to take a subway ride in order to see a Black play?

Bullins: I guess so. They've been doing Black writers' works down here for a number of years, so I guess they had some Black people coming down here to see what was done.

Imp: Do you think that the audience has changed much in what it expects of the play and the playwright over the last, say, ten years?

Bullins: Well, you know, when I do a play, people still come in the doors and sit in the seats and they like or they don't like it. They're just so many people to me.

Imp: How concerned are you with whether the audience understands whatever point you were trying to make, or idea you are trying to convey, in presenting the play?

Bullins: Well, I don't know if I convey that many ideas in my plays. I try to write the story and if somebody can see that, well, then he'll see the story and everything else in it. And if they get it, they get it, and if they don't, I guess it wasn't for them.

Imp: Do you think that any of your plays has a specific theme?

Bullins: Well, I guess the theme comes up, whatever that is.

Imp: What kinds of themes do you think you've been examining?

Bullins: Well, I've only written one play, in my memory, that had a theme. That was "The Taking of Miss Janie," and that theme was the destruction of illusion during the sixties. That was the theme. And I don't know if everyone that left the theater had that in mind. "Oh, he was talking about the destruction of illusion in the sixties....."

Imp: People seem to be focusing on different aspects of "The Taking of Miss Janie" with wide differences of opinion on what the play was about and what it was saying. Do you feel that the writer has to take responsibility for whether his work is understood?

Bullins: Well, the writer doesn't propose any responsibility on an object or his goals by writing the thing.

Imp: What motivates you to write?

Bullins: To play God, to create. To make money (laughs). To be famous (laughs). Meet a lot of women so I can fall in love with them (laughs). Usual motivitations for me.

Imp: Do you find drama the form of writing that you like to deal with the most?

Bullins: Well, theater seems to be the most compatible form for me so far.

Imp: How has your work been influenced in terms of theatrical styles and other playwrights?

Bullins: Well, I had written "How Do You Do," my first play, and then became aware of Baraka's work. But his work did have an impact on me, in my subsequent work. But I just write in my own style, I guess.

Imp: How would you define your style?

Bullins: Bullinesque. (laughs)

Imp: I was especially interested in the use of time, in terms of the shifting back and forth, in "The Taking of Miss Janie." Do you expect to make more use of that type of structure?

Bullins: Sure. I mean, "The Devil Catchers" and "The Psychic Pretenders", I set them in the future. So that had a theme that transcended time. So I stretch my work towards certain things.

Imp: How do you think your new base at the Public Theater will affect your work?

Bullins: Well, my work is writing plays and trying to develop some writers for the Public Theater, the New York Shakespeare Festival, the American playwrighting thing, discovering scripts and talent and all that. I think I'll be quite successful. I'm generally successful at anything I go after, set my mind to.

Imp: How much should the playwright take into account the audience he's writing for? Do you feel that the meaning of a play can change with the audience?

Bullins: Sure. That's all a facet of art. The audience changes. If you do a play for the Daughters of the American Revolution and for the sisters at the Abyssinian Baptist Church, you get a different audience in each. You may think you have the

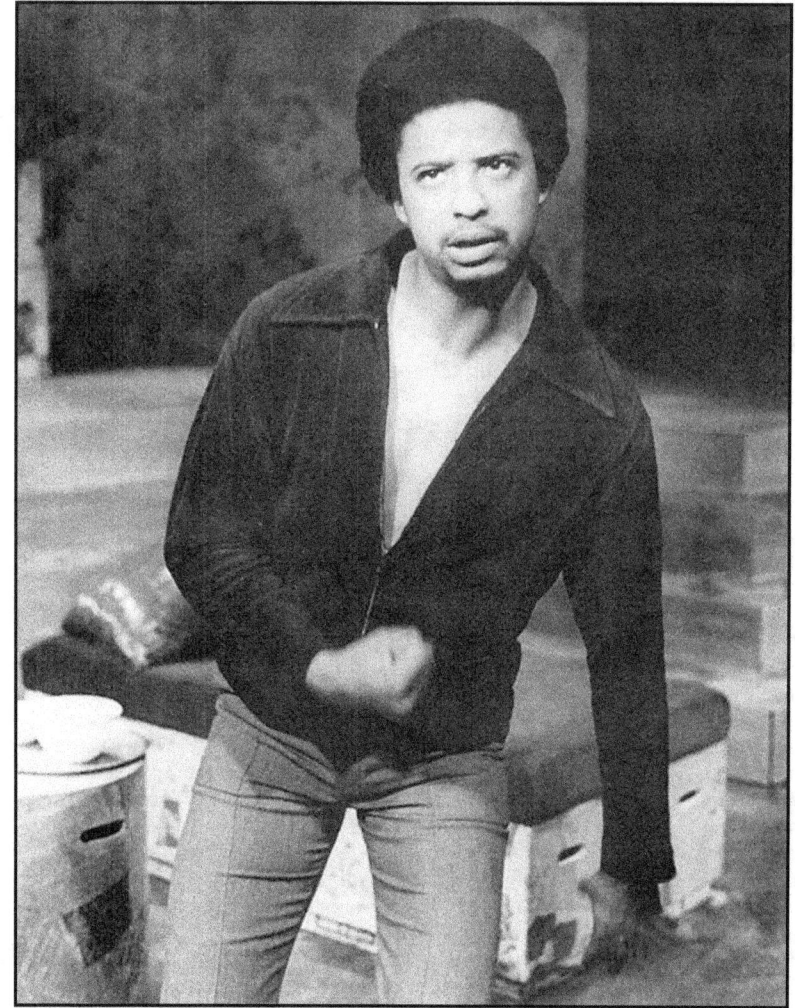

Photo by Bert Andrews   Adeyemi Lythcott in the *The Taking of Miss Janie.*

same play, but when it gets in the room and starts working, it changes. It's one of the excitements about theater. You never know what's going to happen. You can have a play running a year and it's different every night, because there are different people in the room and you wonder what's going to happen.

Imp: Do you think that the audience can change the meaning of the play through their reactions to characters and what they represent in terms of symbols?

Bullins: Sure. The audience will definitely identify with what they want to identify with or shut off or cut off.....

Imp: Do you think the writer has to worry about that?

Bullins: No, I think the writer should worry about writing plays, or writing the work. I spent a lot of time in one period of my life thinking about the audience I was gonna develop and the audience I was going to reach and how to do it for the audience. But the audience isn't a mindless lump that just sits there and lets things be done to it. They either come or they won't come or they might be a completely different set of people than you thought. Some of my plays that were done for a very strictly Black audience were done in Hungary or Czechoslovakia, and I know they were not being done for Black people over there. So people take the plays and take the work, and it gets done.

Imp: But doesn't the writer still have to accept responsibility for the play?

Bullins: No, he doesn't have any responsibility. What responsibility does an artist have? You don't have any responsibility. Not if you really think about it. Because any idea, any set of rules, any standards, from an artist's point of view, can be changed, can be broken, can be refuted.

Imp: Do you think plays that set out to make specific social statements have any effect?

Bullins: Sure. It has an effect on those people who are listening. People of a certain persuasion love didacticism. It reaffirms everything that they believe.

Imp: So the writer won't reach anybody but those who already share his viewpoint?

Bullins: Very few others. How many people you know have been changed by a play? Either they agreed with it or they didn't agree with it. It doesn't change anybody

from a Democrat to a Republican; nor are they going to be anti-American or be against the war because of the play. They saw the play, the *play* moved them, not because of its political dialectic...I mean, you can put anything in a play. All the great truths, and all the political programs and everything else in it. But it's dependent upon the artist how well it comes over, how well it's done. And that's what moves people.

Imp: Do you feel that ideas can accumulate in a person's mind over a period of time....

Bullins: Sure...

Imp: and change the way the person thinks?

Bullins: In terms of their understanding, attitudes, and ideals, yeah. I guess you can force-feed them, pump all this new knowledge into them and you get a new animal. But I don't think with isolated plays you can counteract what the media does and what everyday life does to people.

Imp: How has your attitude about your position as a writer in relationship to society changed since you were associated with Black House and New Lafayette? What kinds of changes have you gone through that would lead you now to these ideas about your writing?

Bullins: Well, I've had a lot of plays done. I've been mildly successful in what I do. I've seen a lot of things come and go. Staunch, rabid, fanatical Black separatists are now talking about integration. All the people who were talking about this when they were putting it down a couple of years ago are talking about that. So I've seen some things, so I guess all that plays a part in where I am now.

Imp: And that's what you were saying in "The Taking of Miss Janie," that these kinds of changes have taken place.

Bullins: Yeah, that's just a picture of the times, a record.

Imp: The 70's, unlike past decades, doesn't seem to have a particular style of its own

Bullins: The '70's is a socially stagnant time. So I guess we'll be remembered for that.

Imp: Do you have any ideas about how long this stagnancy will last?

Bullins: Well, they keep on putting those boobs and assholes in the White House, and they keep on giving all that money to the Army. It'll change, but I don't know if it'll be that better.

Imp: But you are optimistic about your work.

Bullins: Well, I keep on writing. I keep on pushing.

Imp: Then, basically the force that makes you write has not been obstructed in any way?

Bullins: No, it hasn't derailed, because I'm still writing. I wonder if anybody reads it, but I'm still writing (laughs).

Imp: How did you feel about winning the New York Drama Critics Circle Award?

Bullins: I was surprised.

Imp: Why were you surprised?

Bullins: Well, I didn't know what it was, and then when I found that it was rated so important and I'd won it, I was surprised.

Imp: So how do you feel about winning it?

Bullins: Where's the money? (laughs)

Imp: Black people are becoming more involved in the Broadway theater scene. "The Wiz" is an example of this. What do you think of the current movement toward Black resources being utilized for Broadway productions?

Bullins: Black resources? Like what?

Imp: Like choreographers, actors...how do you feel about that whole social phenomenon?

Bullins: I don't look at that like raw resources, like money. But the artists are there, sure. Well, Blacks will now. You know, out of the thirty something theaters that are Broadway theaters, maybe three or four this season will have Black productions. So Blacks have a segment of that, and that will continue.

Imp: Some people say that Broadway has been enriched by a revitalizing surge of energy from this increased Black involvement.

Bullins: Well, this is one of the best years in history for Broadway. Blacks have participated, contributed to that also, but it would still be a great year, one of the best years if it wasn't for Black participation and productions. If there's any "enriching" to be done, I hope I'm "enriched" somewhere down the line because I've put in a lot of time and I've developed a lot of work. I don't know. I don't know if there's anything to get up in a sweat about. It's happening. It's observable. What can you do?

Imp: Do you still feel that you are the best living American playwright?

Bullins: Best living?

Imp: Yes.

Bullins: Oh, let me see. What have I seen lately? Nope, I'm still about

Cont'd on page 53

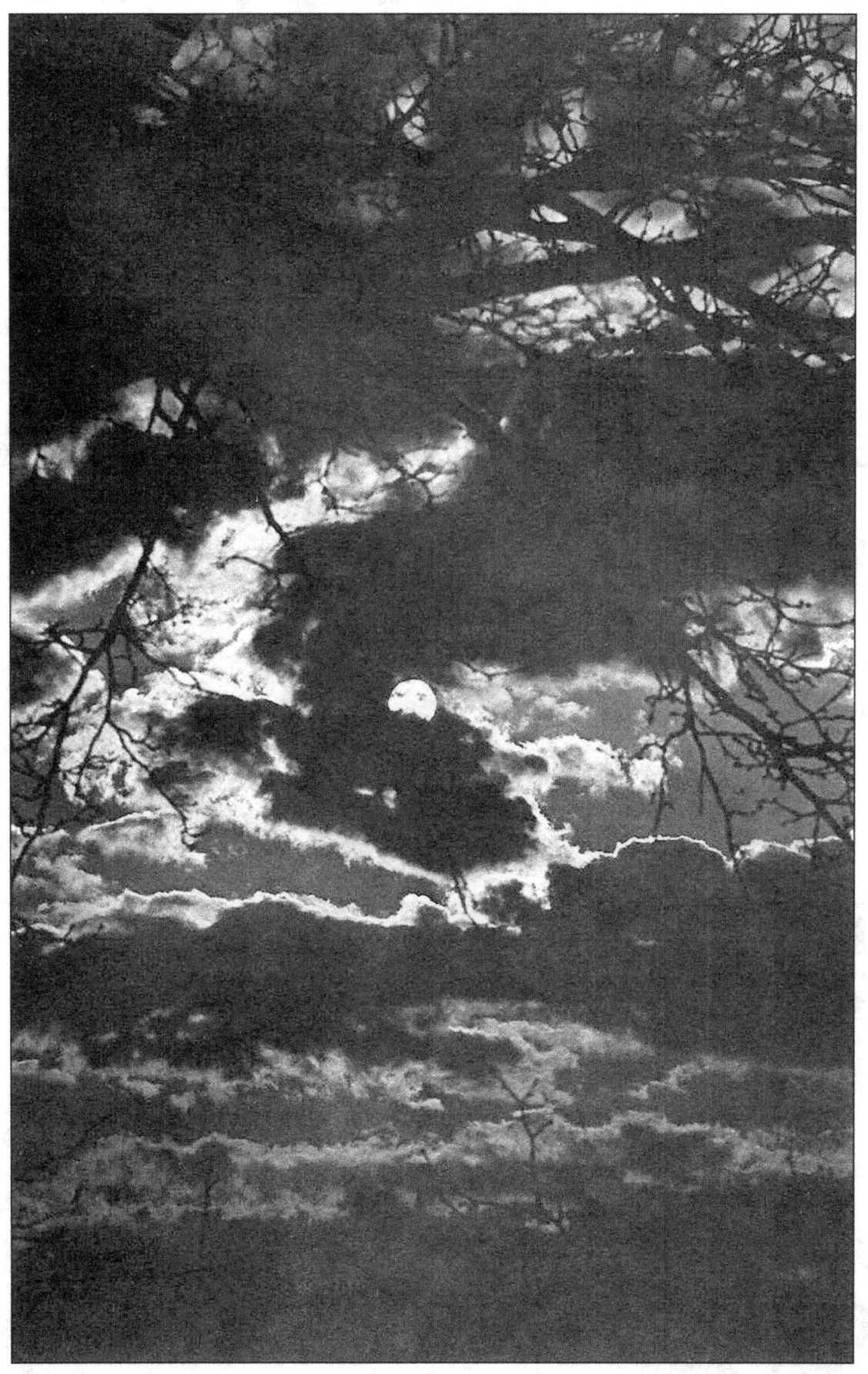

by Leslie Jean-Bart

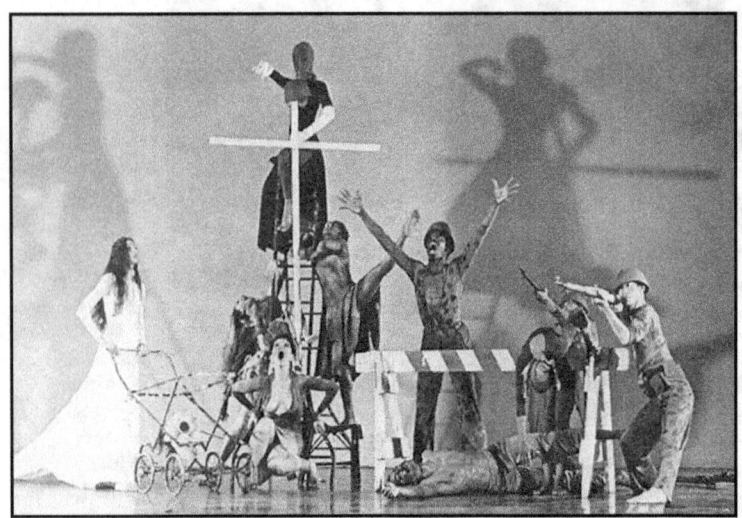

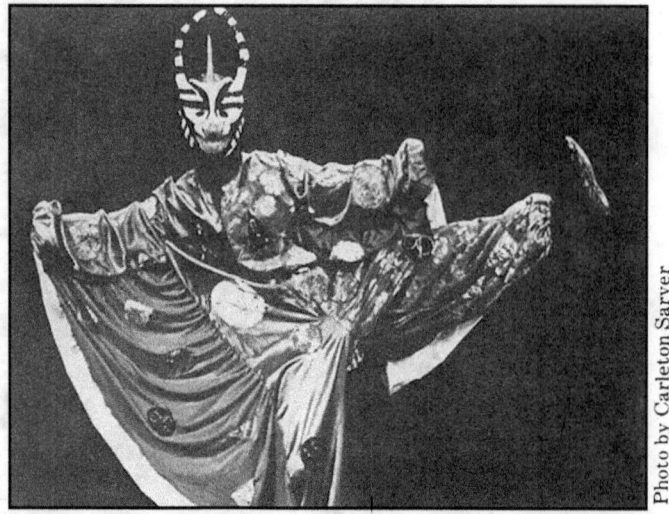

Left page (clockwise):
Top left, Eleo Pomare Dance Co.; top right, Ballet Hispanico of New York; center, La Rocque Bey Dancers and Drummers; bottom right, Luis Rivera Co. (Barbara Picardo); bottom left, George Faison Universal Dance Experience.

Right page (clockwise):
Top left, Sounds in Motion; top right, Rod Rodgers Dance Co.; bottom right, Alvin Ailey City Center Dance Theatre (left, Sara Yarborough; right, Judith Jameson); bottom right, Dance Theatre of Harlem, Inc. (left, Paul Russell; right, Laura Brown); center, Pepsi Bethel Authentic Jazz Dance Theatre.

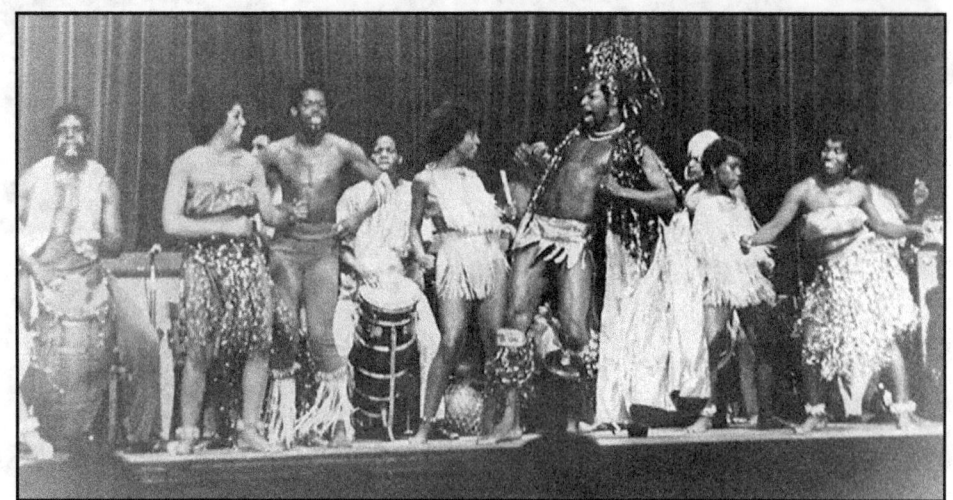

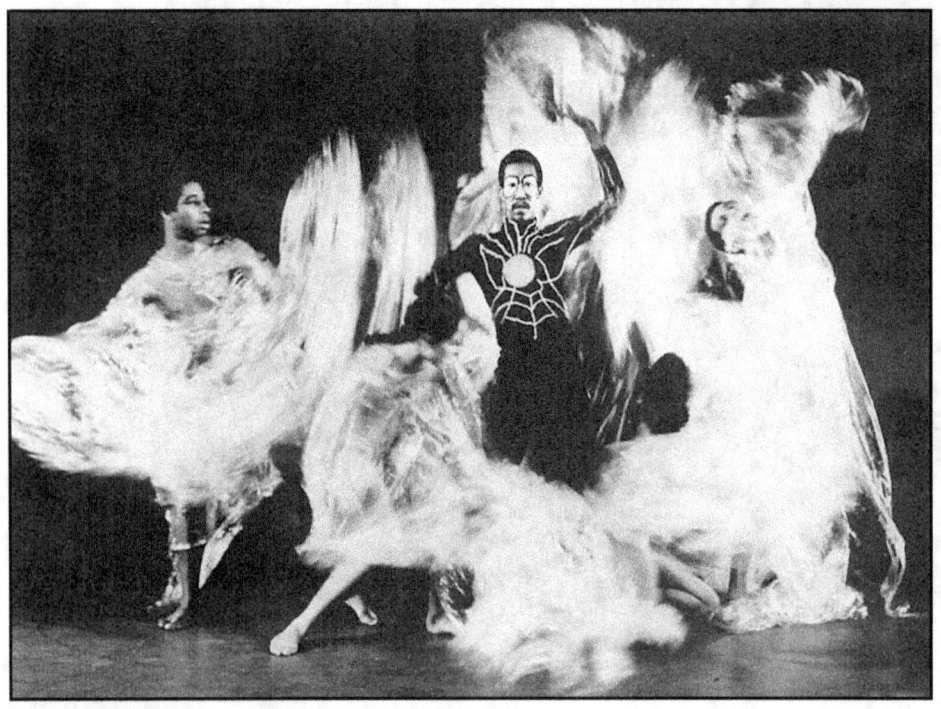

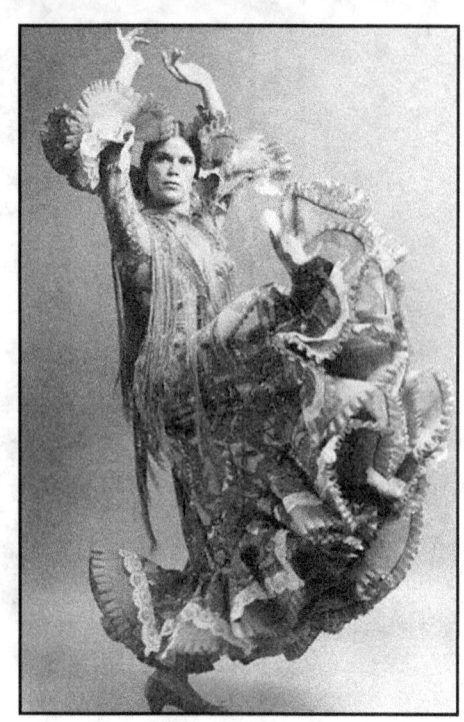

DANCE

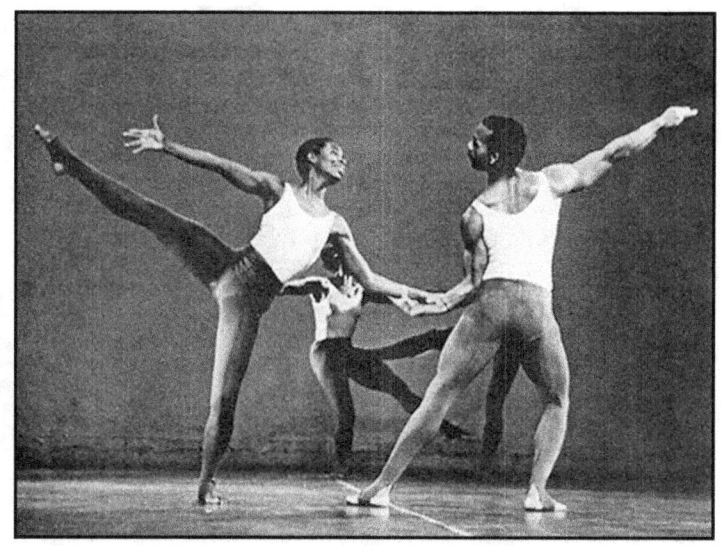

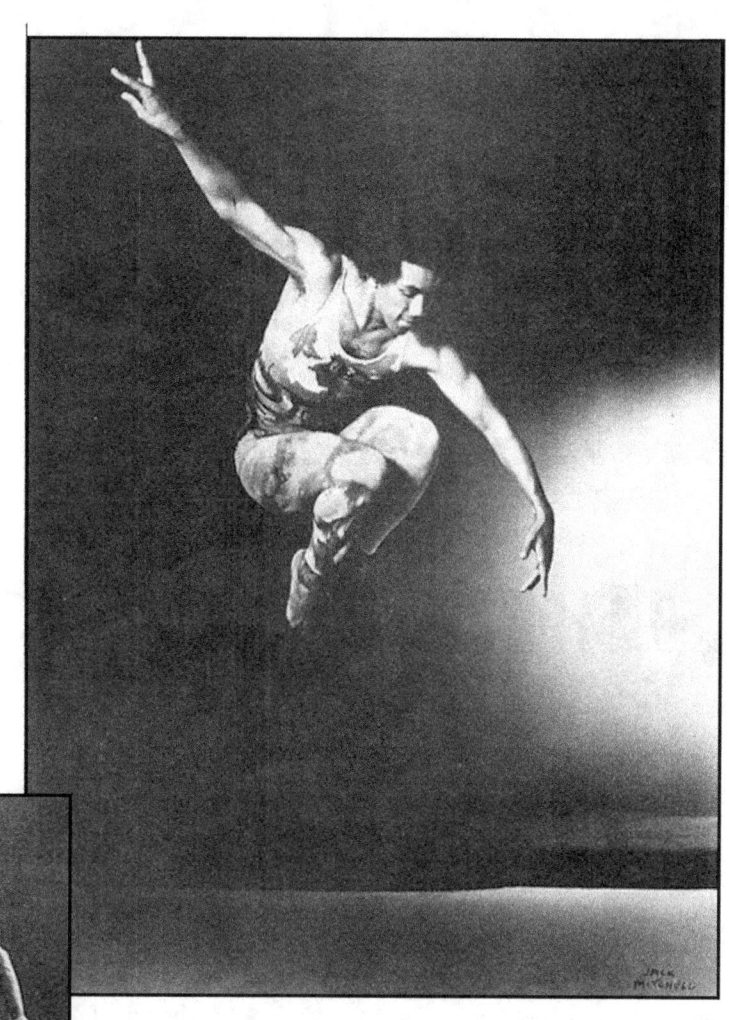

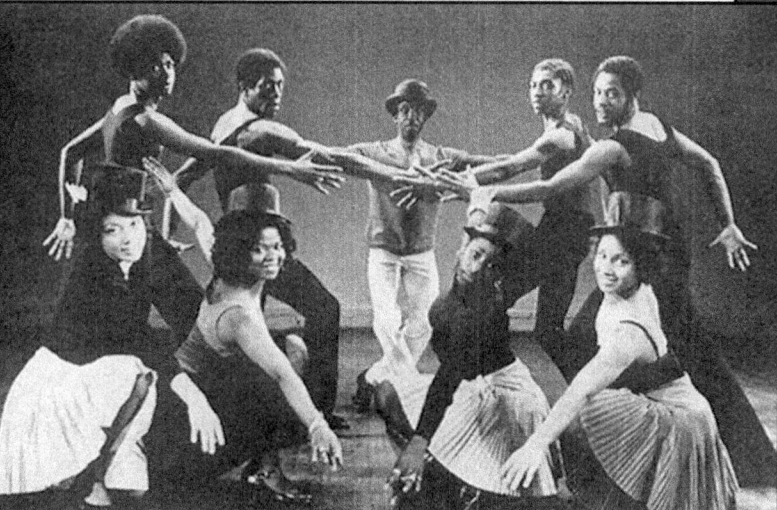

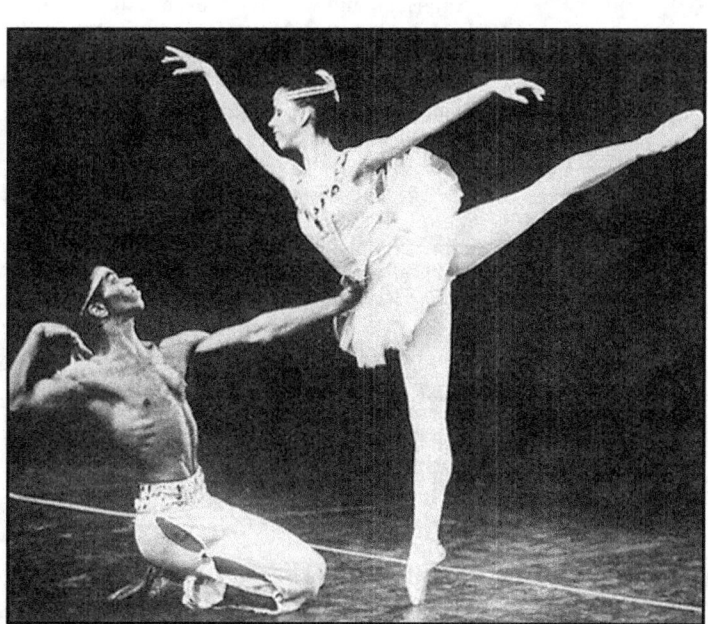

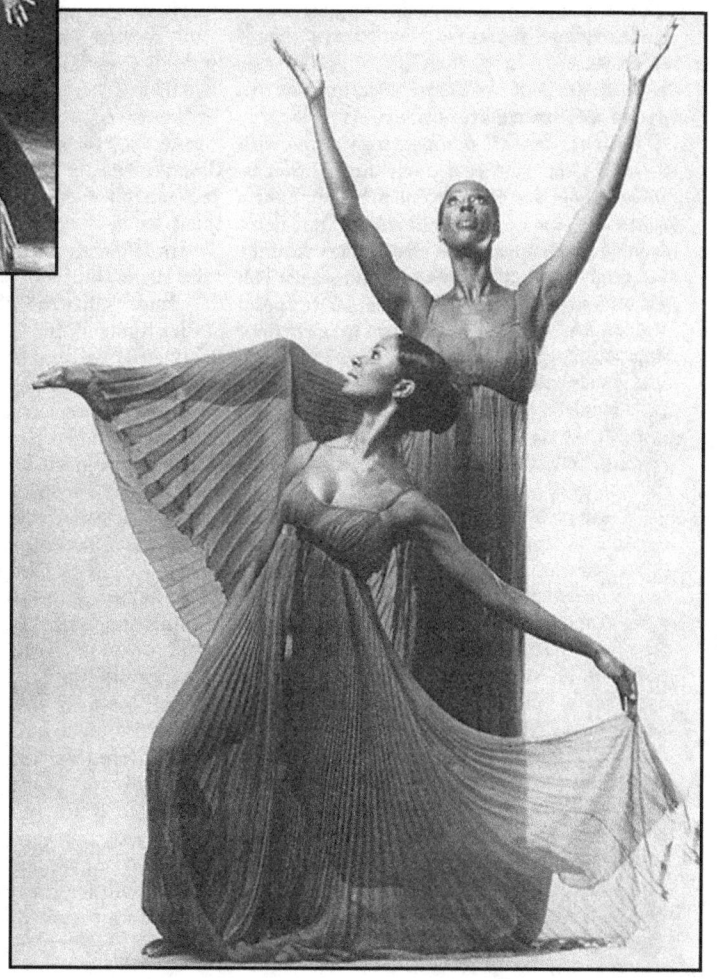

Photo by Martha Swope

REFLECTIONS OF John Oliver Killens

Novelist, Essayist, Playwright

by Bob Bryan

Impressions: James Baldwin is quoted as saying, "The Western World has created me, given me my name, has hidden my truth as a permanent historical fact." In your opinion, is it possible for a people, Black people who have undergone Western acculturation, to evolve an African literature?

Killens: Well, I don't entirely agree with Jimmy. I feel that we are African Americans. I feel that the most scientific and precise term for us is "Afro-American." I don't believe that you can live in a country for four hundred years and some of its culture not rub off on you. I think that we are Africans and we are Americans. The African takes care of what our heritage is, and the American takes into consideration that we've been here for four hundred years. So that I think that we are Afro-Americans.

Imp: What can Afro-American culture be defined as?

Killens: I would define Afro-American culture as people who have a heritage in Africa and four hundred years in this country. For example, Afro-American music has Afro-American rhythms, but its lyrical content is very American, its idiom. Another example is Afro-American language, which I sometimes call Afro-Americanese. So my definition of Afro-American culture is a mixture of African culture and American. It takes into consideration the last four or five hundred years of whoever is the influencer of a heritage going back four or five thousand years. I don't see how you can just call it one. My own opinion is that for a long time Black people denied their African heritage. During the 1920's and again during the 1960's there

was a step-up of identification with Africa, which was very good. I think the writers played a role in this. Malcolm played a role in this, because for a long time if you said to someone that they should go to Africa, they would tell you that they hadn't lost anything in Africa. Malcolm said, "You lost your mind in Africa." So what I'm saying is, in order to compensate for once denying Africa, there is a tendency to jump over four hundred years that we've spent here. They've been heroic years, fighting the most vicious system on this planet.

Imp: What writers do you think have really personified that which you would define as "cultural writers?"

Killens: Well, I think a lot of people. Sterling Brown comes to mind. In the 1920's he was writing what some people call Negro Renaissance period. Sterling would probably call it the Negro Renaissance period. Calling it the Harlem Renaissance period makes it seem as if nothing is happening anywhere else but in New York. But that's not true. I would say Sterling, Langston Hughes, Arna Bontemps, of the 1920's, all these people extend over time. In the 1960's, Langston Hughes did. So did Arna Bontemps. I think LeRoi Jones in the '60's, and Ellison, and James Baldwin himself. He's right, he's a product of America, and that can be taken negatively or positively. I think that the history of Black people in this country has been a very courageous history, something to be proud of. We have been under circumstances that no other people have had to face, and we've survived. Matter of fact, we've survived and contributed to the culture of

this country and Africa. I was watching this TV program one morning and I saw some South Koreans. They were demonstrating against their despotic government, and they were singing in Korean, "We Shall Overcome." Goes to show you the impact that Black people have had on the entire world; wherever people have struggled, they've identified with Black people.

But we tend to leap over these four hundred years, that produced people like Denmark Vesey, Nat Turner, Paul Robeson, Malcolm; look over this and deny them and identify completely with Africa. I think we can do both. As I said before, we are Afro-American and we have reason to be proud of both our heritage here as well as the one in Africa. To deny one and to claim the other is, to me, a misfortune. That's what happened to some in the Sixties. They didn't want to, or cared very little what was written about Denmark Vesey, Nat Turner. It took William Styron to write about Nat Turner. He defamed Nat Turner in the book. We got out a book which featured the responses of ten black writers to Styron's book. But one of us should have written a book about Nat Turner in the first place. Realizing that, I was one of the contributors. I did a book about Denmark Vesey called *Great Getting Up Morning*. Harriet Tubman and Sojourner Truth were also heroes who faced situations that were insurmountable.

Imp: And when you look at it, you must take into consideration the actual social situation of the times.

Killens: That's right. I know that Africans are not deceived. Africans know that we are Afro-Americans and they are very glad that we identify with them. But they also sense that we are brothers from America, and that's what we are.

Imp: In response to Styron's "Nat Turner," you say that the great American tragedy is Black tragedy, that we Black folks live with tragedy. We inhale tragedy with our every breath. Could you expand upon what you meant there?

Killens: I think that a sense of tragedy has been lacking in some of the writing. A tragic person is quite different from a pathetic person who just sits around feeling sorry for himself. We have been depicted as pathetic people, but I think we are a people of tragedy, of paradox. Most people came to this country seeking freedom. We were brought here in chains; that's the paradox. Martin Luther King said, "It's difficult to tell a people to pick themselves up by the bootstraps when they don't have any shoes." But the Jews, Italians, and other immigrants that came here, they caught hell, too. There's no question about it. But for them to tell us, look where we went, look at what we've done, they came here seeking freedom, we came here in chains.

Imp: A lot of people have said to me, "Well, I'm not into Black literature, because it seems to be so negative." In that the work is so negative, the characters are stereotyped, things like that. Is that caught within the genre of tragedy or is tragedy necessarily an extract of a negative environment? For example, if someone is considering writing a Black love story in the context of this social, political situation here, could it be a positive love story but still considered negative becuase of the environment?

Killens: Well, I think so. It would be a positive love story. I think it should be. I don't see tragedy as a negative thing. I don't see, for example, Shakespeare's work as negative, but what I was saying is that a tragedy envisions epic hereos, people who stood up and fought. I wouldn't consider Paul Robeson a pathetic man. I consider Paul Robeson a man of tragedy, but a great hero. The most powerful monolithic establishment in the whole world, and he fought it. He made a conscious decision to do so. Malcolm's life was a tragedy, but I don't see it as negative. I don't think that anyone could say that Malcolm's life was negative. I mean, he came up the essence of Black life in this country, went through all of this.

Imp: He was a victim of it.

Killens: And he transcended it. That, to me, is positive. So if you write about Malcolm, if you write the tragedy, if you write about Martin Luther King, you must write about heroes. Malcolm or Martin, even Medgar Evans, chose their weapons and decided to fight. Whereas other people made accommodation with the establishment in order to live good. I don't think that they're heroic. You can write about a man who has made his peace with the establishment. Some people might think that that's a positive story, but I don't think so. I think that the heroes of Black people are really tragedies. I see tra-

gedies as positive. But my criticisms of some of the writings, I don't like to call names, they've written about the nooks and crannies, corners of Black life. Black people are really an epic in this country. Very few writers have seized from this the epic and made people proud of themselves.

Imp: In 1952, in *Freedomways*, you wrote a commentary about Ralph Ellison's *Invisible Man*. Do you remember that piece? What did you think about the novel, *Invisible Man*?

Killens: Ellison, I feel, is a tremendous craftsman. He's a brilliant writer. I appreciate that. I probably learned something from his writing. He's master and he's an Afro-American. What I didn't like was the lack of growth in his main character. Now this is it, don't think this is what I said at the time, because that was when I was very less mature. But part of the reaction to Ellison was probably a gut reaction. What I would say today is that Ellison's a brilliant writer who won the National Book Award for all the wrong reasons. But Herbert Hill of the NAACP has become the expert on Negro literature. He's a white man and, to paraphrase him, he said that Ellison has transcended his race and gone into the mainstream of literature. I feel he got the National Book Award because it was during a period of McCarthyism when a lot of red-baiting was going on. Ellison seemed to place the burden of the exploitation of Black people on what he called the brotherhood . Which would make the establishment very fond of him.

But the essential criticism I had was that his character didn't grow. I have problems with the whole symbol of invisibility. Invisible to who, the white man? In the end of the novel, Ellison's main character found out that he was looking in the wrong place for invisibility. As a matter of fact, one of the problems of Black people is that we have a high degree of visibility. I think people might say, well, you didn't dig what Ellison was saying. That he was talking about, every time a white person sees a black person, he sees a black person, he doesn't know the difference...

Imp: You mean like a stereotype?

Killins: Yeah. But he knows the difference. The white man plays a lot of tricks. He always knows the difference between Booker T. Washington and W. E. B. DuBois. He knows the difference between the loyal slaves and Denmark Vesey, what they called, "the bad niggers," the field Negro and the house Negro. In any event, it is not our concern what the white man sees. At the end of the book, he was still looking for this white man to recognize him. So I would have liked to have seen some growth in his character. But his character, at the end of the book, is still reaching out for that recognition from the white man.

Imp: At the same time, there are characters or people like that who are wrapped up in that.

Killens: You know, it's hard to separate Ellison's character from the novelist. What

impact is Ellison trying to have over the readership? That a person must look for acceptance in this way? I don't think that's what I would like to have seen. But then, this is writing his book. It's not important how the white man sees the main character. It's how the character sees himself that's important. In Richard Wright's *Native Son*, there are quite a few differences, but also similarities. I never could get through my mind why Bigger killed a white woman accidentally, but killed Bessie deliberately. After all, he loved Bessie. I couldn't reconcile that; I still don't understand what that meant. What was Richard Wright saying in the handling of these two situations? There are some similarities between the two books because they came out of the same period, the same era. There was this identification with everything white. We had not yet evolved. I think that Ellison was s step ahead of Richard Wright, in that he had a character that was thinking. I don't know if anyone can consider Bigger to be a great thinker. Bigger seemed to be flustered by this big, white *system*. He affirms his manhood by killing Bessie. Bigger scared the hell out of a few white people for a time. White people sometimes pretend to be frightened. Like the so-called race riots that I would call police riots. Because I think that some of them were plotted, in police stations, to try out new weapons on the "natives." It's really interesting the way *Native Son* is, I believe, the only Black novel ever to become a "Book of the Month." *Invisible Man* is the only Black novel to have been given the National Book Award.

Imp: How about Wright's *The Outsider?* Is there a transcendence, an evolvement in the personality from the beginning to the end?

Killens: When Richard Wright was over there in Europe, surrealism was the thing. But what sticks in my mind was at one point when the character, Cross Daemon, goes to the manager in this apartment house and sees these two white men fighting about him. He kills them both. I think he's saying that no white people are any good. I think that Wright's best writings were *Uncle Tom's Children* and *Twelve Million Black Voices*. And that's very interesting to me. In *Twelve Million Black Voices*, which was, I think, a Black historical poetic essay, a black mother stands in front of her gingerbread shack. This is in Mississippi. Her son leaves her at the house, to go up North, and a love goes with him that transcends any of the laws of the white man. No matter what he does out there, he knows he can always come home to be loved, fed and protected. Now, about seven or eight years later, Wright wrote a book called *Black Boy* in which, to paraphrase, he said, "Look back at my life, back then, filled with emotion, Black people's emotion, like love and hate : There is quite a big difference from the other statements, and this is autobiographical. These are not characters, but Wright, himself, speaking. I don't know what happened in eight or ten years that would make such a turn-over. From one point, love transcended everything, but ten years later there is a lack of love.

I think Richard Wright became disillusioned with the Communist Party, and when you become disillusioned, you have to have some meaning in your life. In one of his poems called, "I'm Black and I've Seen Black Hands," he said at the end of the poem that, to paraphrase him again, "One day," and this is a stage, maybe, "there'll be a day of blood struggle, but white and black workers will join hands to fight against the establishment." Now those are not the exact words, but the meaning is there. I think that Wright lost faith in this statement. I don't think that he had enough faith in Black people to sustain him. He went off to Europe and he couldn't come back.

Imp: What do you see as the whole vehicle out of the immediate, fist-raising social situation? Do you see it as the "revolution" of the Sixties, or do you see other ways of effectuating change in this country?

Killens: Well, I think the best contribution to this has been a book written by Chancellor Williams. It's called *The Destruction of Black Civilization*, and I reviewed it for *New Directions*, a magazine at Howard University. This book covers 45 B.C. up to the present. He says that the first white people who came to Africa were from Asia, and that they came with three hundred and four hundred year plans. They knew that the benefits of their infiltration of Africa would not be realized in their time or their children's time or their children's children's children's time, and that eventually that area which used to be totally black, which is called Egypt, would be white. Too much money, energy and human resources was expended on the Pyramids, temples and monuments for the dead, and not enough was used for the black man's prosperity for generations yet unborn. I did a piece for *The Black Scholar* called, "Wanted: Some Long-Distance Runners." I think that it's very interesting that we have produced some of the most magnificent athletes that the world has ever seen, but very few long-distance runners. If we look at the relays, we take off like a bat out of Hell, we always take those 100 yard dashes...

Imp: Isn't that sort of an economic thing, too, people being forced to do it for money? Aren't we involved in a political situation? We are forced to live in Harlem by economics. So aren't we reacting to the situation instead of going beyond the situation in order to take control of it?

Killens: I think that's true. I think that the reasons that we don't have long-distance runners, planners, is that we've been forced by the society to live a hand-to-mouth kind of existence. So our planning has a tendency to be hand-to-mouth. But it ain't going to win no long race. It's true, it's a rationalization, an explanation. Somehow, I believe, we have to transcend it, and I don't think that moving out of Harlem is the answer. Most black people are living in the Harlems of the USA because they need a job, and that's what Malcolm was all about. He was about changing those Harlems of the USA from citadels of despair to monuments of hope. As far as

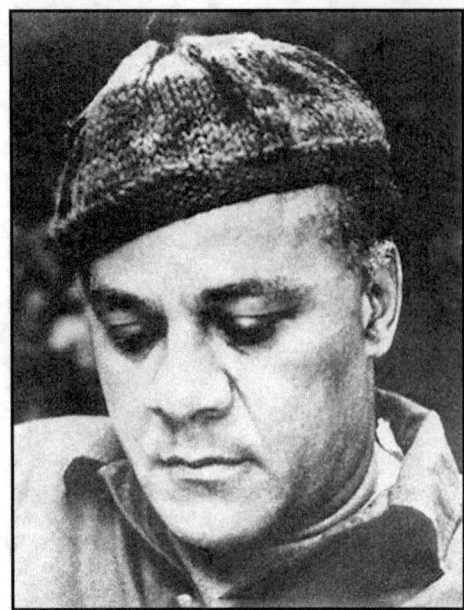

Photo by Willard Moore

I'm concerned, that's what controlling the schools is all about: community control of economics. I think that while you work for a total change of the system, you have to work to change the situation of black folks. So people who talk foolishly of settling for nothing but the whole thing, that's good, but the dialetics of it...one of the great revolutionaries of this century said that we cannot arrange a revolution, and that's general knowledge. Revolution, especially bloody revolution, means people get killed, and people will take all kinds of shit until the last minute, they'll make all kinds of arrangements to accommodate, before they run out into the street.

Blacks are always out front, but very few are in the mile. Long distance requires planning, pacing, discipline and a belief that you can win in the long run. I don't think that there's any easy answer to your question. I think that we are under the illusion that one stroke, one hundred yard dashes like the sit-ins, bus boycotts, that this would overthrow the establishment, that this would turn the country around. The freedom rides, then the sit-ins; these were one hundred yard dashes, sprints, but there was nobody at that point planning and pacing to put these things together, to make a fundamental change in our circumstances. And I'm not preaching gradualism, but I'm just looking factually. In one fell swoop we cannot overthrow the greatest amassment of power the world has ever seen. This country is so powerful, it makes the Roman Empire look like an exercise in tiddly-winks.

Imp: Would you extend the analogy of the Roman Empire in terms of its fall?

Killens: Well, I see a lot of evidence. I see decadence. I mean, all you have to do is walk down Forty-second Street and you see decadence, everything. A lot of similarities. So-called sexual revolution, tremendous upsurge of homosexuality. All these are evidence of decadence. But people are anxious to jump on the ship that's sinking. We want to be just as decadent. Down on 42nd Street you see black

dudes hustlin', pimpin' and everything else. Trying to get on this boat, that's sinking.

Imp: How does the writer go out, to quote you, "to explore the truth of man's relationship to man?"

Killens: First of all, he has to do everything possible to know himself. Not who he wants to be, but who he actually is. He must always be looking at himself. I don't mean spending time in analysis or anything like that. But really trying to know himself, because if he doesn't know himself, he can't know Black people. He must know himself first, then he looks at the society. He has to do some thinking about how he relates to the society. Some people ask me, "How long did it take you to write 'Youngblood'?" And I say sometimes, "All my life." So you look at these things and you come to some fundamental conclusions, and these conclusions should be reflected in your writing. The best writers are out to change the world. Every time you sit down at a typewriter, try to make it a fit place for human habitation. The only way you can do this is by becoming more aware of yourself through your relationship to the rest of the world, contributing that understanding to people who read you. That is the last resort before they run out into the streets and shoot. The last resort, for almost every people.

People will rationalize, will do anything before they run out there in the streets and shoot (laughter). To say that you'll run out there and shoot is to say that the man doesn't have guns. I was telling a group of kids to do like the Indians, run out there and yell, and you'll get wasted. There will always be white people who will sell the weapons. By the time you get ready to use them, they are outdated and the man's weaponry is sophisticated..that's what they did to the Indians. The white man was selling the weapons, but by the time the Indians got ready to use them, the white man had repeater rifles and wiped them out. So I think that the first thing we have to do is to get our heads together. I know that I spoke to a group out there in San Francisco about ten years ago. Brothers were talking about going out there and shooting Whitey. But they had no concrete plans for doing anything.

I think one of the big problems is unity. Back to your question, you got to get Black people to love each other again. People are not going to die for people who they don't love. I see a growing self-contempt, even among our writers. I see us accepting the white people's word, "nigger." One brother said to me, "You're one brother I've really wanted to meet, you're really my nigger." I said, "No, I'm not your nigger, I'm not the white man's nigger." (Laughter) I'm not anybody's nigger. I'm just my own man. I definitely don't want anybody calling my grandchildren niggers, affectionately or not, and I don't want them to grow up accepting the use of the word. See, one has to do one of two things. The position that the white man takes is that I, a black man, am inferior. If you don't accept that, then you have to say that the whole establishment is full of shit and sick and needs to be changed. I have black leaders say things like, "He's a good President, he's just weak on the question of the Negro." That complete denial of yourself, to say that, is crazy, sick. What I'm saying is that once a writer comes to grips with that, then he questions everything. He questions every aspect of this society. If I do not accept the fact that I am inferior, there must be something fundamentally wrong with the system that denies me. Not just one phase of it is wrong, because I am the center of the universe, I am who I am, the man who cried I am. Once you come to grips with that, you question every facet of this establishment, which was based on slavery. It's not easy, but I do think that once you denounce the fact that the whole ideology of you being a sub-human being, once you say that I am, you have to question the very aspect of this society that has denied you.

Imp: What do you consider to be the function of Black critics?

Killens: I think their responsibility is to criticize constructively. I tend to be my own worst critic because I re-write and re-write.

Imp: You are working on a new novel about Alexander Pushkin. Can you tell us a little bit about him?

Killens: Alexander Pushkin is undoubtedly, in the minds of the Russian people, the most important writer that the Russian people have ever produced. Now this comes as a shock to some people because when they think of Russian writers, they think of Dostoevsky, Tolstoy and Turgenev, but people never think of Pushkin. Pushkin was a hero in Imperial Russia. Just about every city in the Soviet Union, which I've visited twice, has a statue of Pushkin. In Moscow they have, in the heart of the town, a place called Pushkin Square. It's a monument to Pushkin. The other thing about Pushkin is that he is an Afro-Russian, which reflects my deep interest in him. His great-grandfather was an Ethiopian who was captured in a war between the Turks and the Ethiopians, at the age of eight, and brought to a harem in Turkey. These were in the days of Peter the Great, in the 1700's, and Russia was a vast empire. Totally agragrian, serfs, feudalistic society. But the Russians had a tremendous inferiority complex vis-a-vis the French. People spoke French in the courts of Russia. It was fashionable throughout Russia to have at least one Negro in your court, either as a footman or buffoon. You were really unsophisticated if you didn't have one. So Peter the Great sent out to all the embassies throughout Europe. "Find me a Negro." The Russian ambassador in Turkey kidnapped Pushkin's great-grandfather, Hannibal, and brought him to the court of Saint Petersburg, which is now Leningrad. Peter was a strapping lad, very intelligent and quick. Peter took a liking to him and became his god-father. The Queen of Poland became his god-mother. He was promoted rapidly from pet to secretary to his Imperial Majesty. When he was about seventeen, Peter the Great took Hannibal to Europe with him on a tour and left him in Paris to get a "classical education," including war engineering. He stayed

there a long time. Peter the Great kept telling him to come back, but he didn't feel that he owed anything to Russia. He didn't ask to be taken there in the first place, and he was having a good time in Paris. So he stayed there until his money and excuses ran out. He went back to Russia, and he didn't realize how fond he was of his godfather until he, Peter the Great, died.

His popularity decreased because there were courtiers who didn't like the idea of this black man being such a big shot in the courts. So he eventually got sent to Siberia, where he spent quite a few years in the salt mines and cold weather. He came back when Elizabeth became empress. She had been his playmate in the court. And his star really went into orbit under her rule and under the rule of Catherine the Great. It is rumored that he and Catherine the Great had a thing, you know. She was a horny empress, as I point out in the book. He was a man, and he was not going to deny her. Besides, he didn't want to go back to Siberia. He married a Russian woman who gave birth to a girl named Madesda. Madesda was considered throughout Russia as the beautiful Creole. She was a beautiful woman. Her skin was mulatto and she was kind of ashamed of her African background. Well, Sergian Pushkin came from a long line of aristocrats, but by this time the money was all gone.

Sergian and Madesda had three children, including Alexander. Alexander came out the darkest. His mother didn't love him because he reminded her too much of her African ancestry, which she was trying to forget. So he spent a lot of time by himself. The only person who ever showed him any love was his nurse, Nyna, who used to tell him stories. She was very proud of her Russian heritage, and she used to tell him stories in the lusty, Russian idiom about the days of Peter the Great. He had a grandmother whose father was Hannibal, Alexander's great-grandfather, and she used to tell Alexander about Peter the Great. Alexander's mother, Madesda, objected to the stories on the grounds that, in her opinion, Hannibal was a "savage" and any tales about him could be garbage. But from the two old women Alexander got an appreciation of Russian history and idiom. He took pride in his ancestors. Unlike Dumas, who wasn't particularly proud of his African ancestry, Pushkin made a point of it in his writings. His mother and father never understood him. He could read all the French literature by the time he was eleven, but then he started moving into the Russian idiom. His father tried to discourage him. Dostoevsky says that Pushkin was the only Russian writer who came close to reflecting the Russian masses; Tolstoy and Turgenev also made an attempt. All the others are like the upper class talking down to the masses. Pushkin reflected the soul of the masses. Without Pushkin, not only wouldn't there be any Russian literature, but there would not have been any national purpose, national will. Dostoevsky was sixteen years old when Pushkin died, and he went on a hunger strike, although he never met Pushkin. Pushkin had

that kind of impact. Pushkin was the first people's poet of Russia. I think our people must know that Africans have made an impact all over the world, not just here and in Africa. I think Pushkin is a fabulous character, and would be a great subject for a fabulous movie. ✿

John Oliver Killens is the author of the following books: *Cotillion; Youngblood; And Then We Heard the Thunder;* and *Black Man's Burden.*

BOB MARLEY

Cont'd from page 35

knowing a banana tree, never knowing a goat, never knowing a donkey, never knowing clean water...never knowing *life.* Africa has the land for I and I, education, opportunities, freedom.Explore Africa...because we have to be strong.

Imp: Again, back to your album NATTY DREAD. There is a side called *So Jah Seh.* I know that JAH means God. How does your concept of JAH differ from, let's say, a Christian's concept of God?

B.M.: The thing about a Christian is that they are almost right...right up to the part where they go into the earth...in a grave. I don't deal with that. They say the gift of God is eternal life...anyway you want it! If you want to die and come back again, great! But, for me personally, in this time, let me know myself. It's flesh, it is material, but I can't make it. When I touch it, I feel it...somehow it's attached to me. I mean to know myself in this flesh, here! This situation and this place cannot go on forever, because this is not natural. To tell you the truth, this is not doing one good thing for people. I was walking down the street awhile ago, my feet got hurt walking down there (asphalt). Something flew in my eye (dust), the noise (honking cars) affected my ear. Everything is just weird...yet this is only New York. ✿

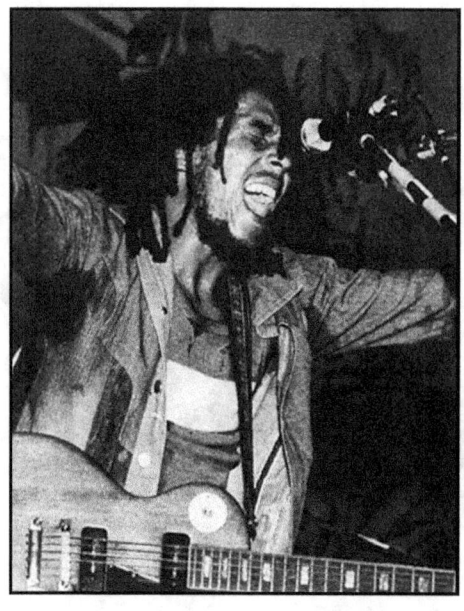

Photo by Harold H. Belgrave

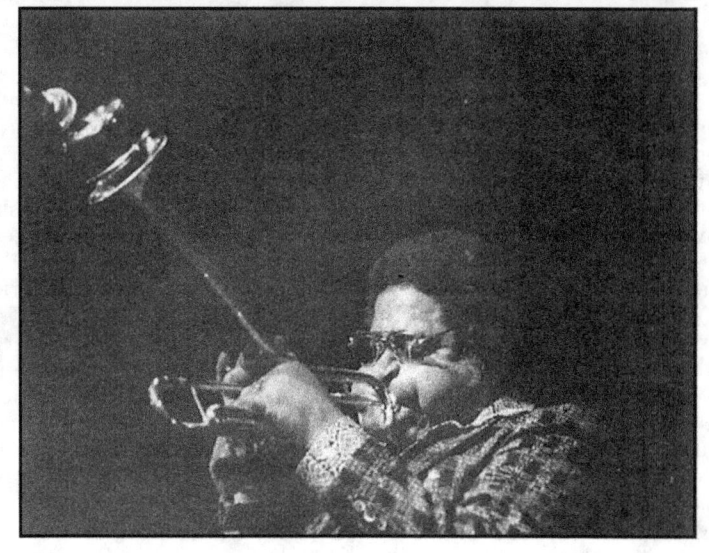

VISIONS OF
BLACK CLASSICAL MUSIC

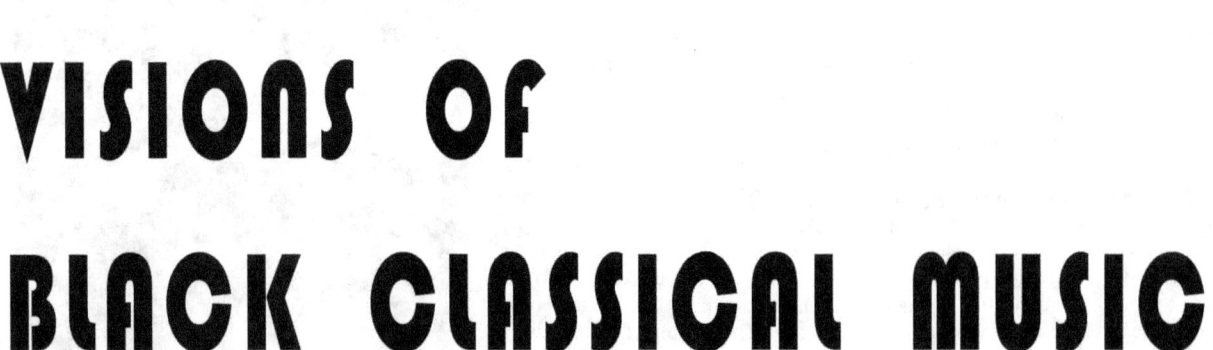

Left page:
Left, **Sun Ra***; top right,* **Leroy Jenkins***;*
bottom right, **Dizzy Gillespie***.*

Right page:
Left, **Charlie Mingus***; top right,* **George
Benson***; bottom right,* **Rahsaan Roland
Kirk***.*

photos by Bob Ellison

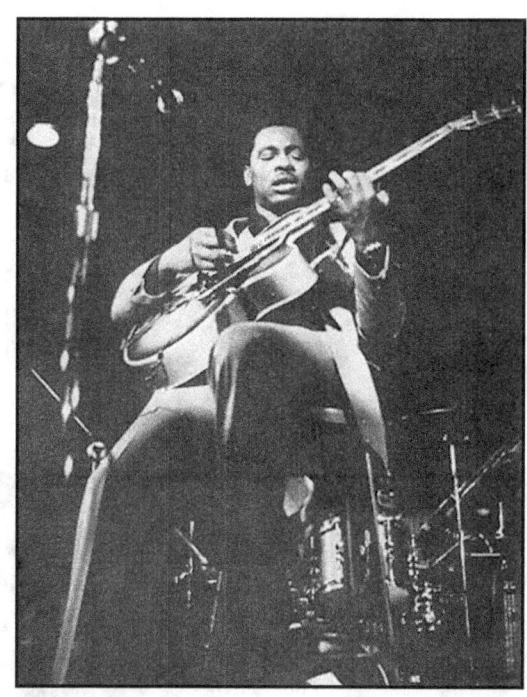

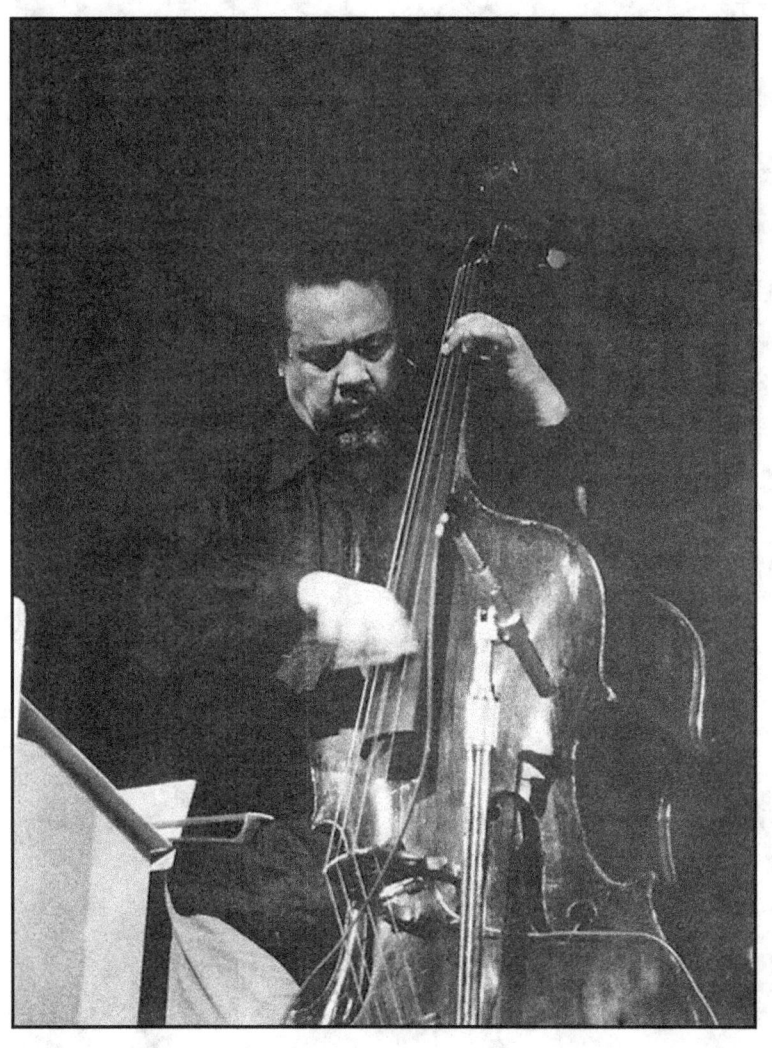

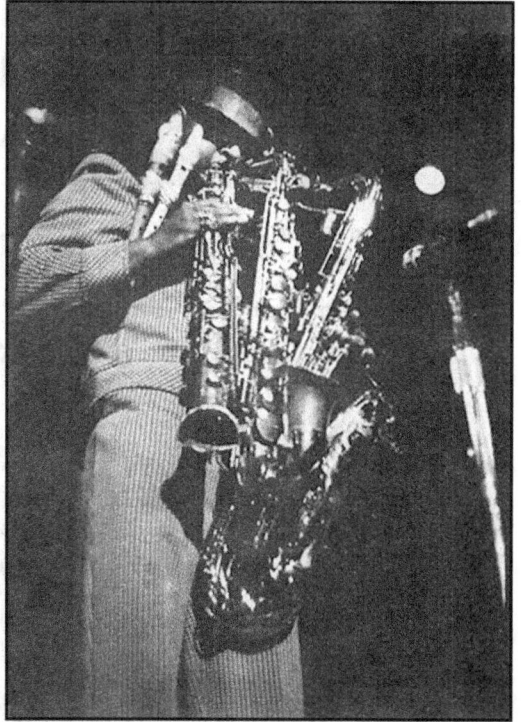

the roots of a jazz singer

JOE LEE WILSON

by Brenda Bailey

Impressions: Well Joe, when did you begin your career as a singer?

Joe: When I was about 5 years old and my first song was *I Know A Secret*.

Imp: From that point on, what was your early musical training and experience?

Joe: Well, I'd sing in all the school performances and operettas, also in the church choir and Sunday school shows.

Imp: So your roots as a singer were in the church?

Joe: Yes, all of my family were religious people.

Imp: And today do you feel those roots as a continual spiritual influence?

Joe: Well, everything is an extension of life. I extend one thing into everything, that way everything is different, but like a continuous chain that is constantly changing and growing.

Imp: I guess that philosophy has really influenced your music.

Joe: Yes, that's how I got into jazz, it's the only music that allows you freedom to be spontaneous.

Imp: Before jazz, what type of music were you into?

Joe: Well, being raised in Oklahoma, I listened to country and western and, later, rhythm and blues. But in my early life and teens, mainly country and western, it's very soulful you know.

Imp: At what point did you decide to dedicate your energies to singing?

Joe: In 1958 I decided to make my living as a jazz singer.

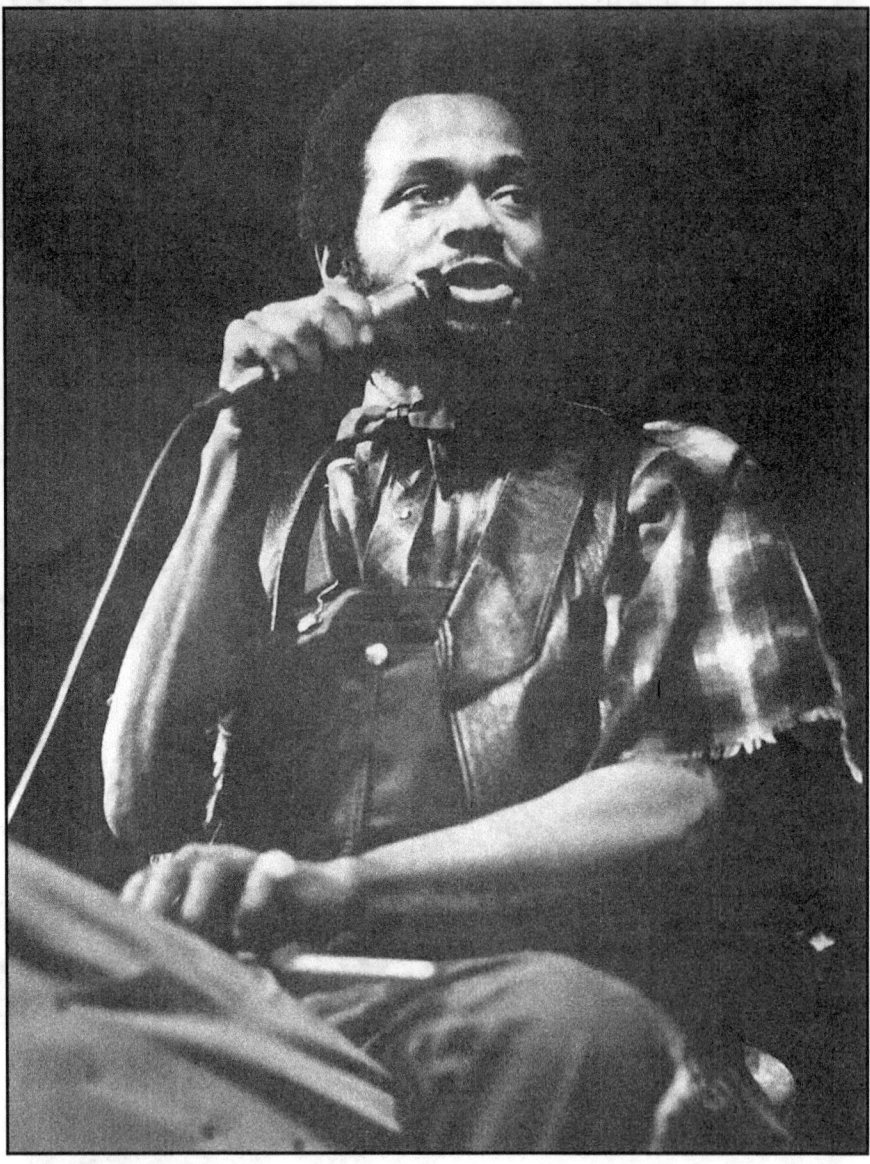

Photo by Bob Ellison

Imp: After that decision, how did you get into music?

Joe: I quit my job as a postal clerk in L.A. and began to sit in at different sets and talent shows. I became the house singer at a club called the Zanzibar in Santa Monica.

Imp: Who influenced your music and moods as a singer at that period?

Joe: Roscoe Weathers, a flautist who worked with Fletcher Henderson. There weren't that many jazz singers at that period and they all influenced me.

Imp: How did you make the change from L.A. to N.Y.?

Joe: L.A was a cool jazz city, not a hard jazz city. I was getting nowhere fast, so I split to S.F. I sat in at Jimbo's, where I met all the great jazz musicians.

Imp: What groups did you work with there?

Joe: I've never been into groups because I'm a loner. My father taught me one thing --being a farmer, you're self-employed, and if you want to make it, you must work for yourself. I really had no intentions of coming to N.Y. I left S.F. for Mexico, where I worked class A clubs for the first time in my life following Nat King Cole and Sammy Davis. In 1962 I met an agent who said he could book me in N.Y. So I came here with the intention of staying two weeks...now it's been twelve years.

Imp: What was your first reaction as a jazz singer in N.Y. City?

Joe: I really felt that I had a distinct sound, that's why I dug jazz. It was an outlet for my type of singing. The sound was as though I was a ventriloquist throwing my voice, and people thought it sounded like I was straining. Even now, that's my trademark as a singer, for people say I sound like I'm straining.

Imp: At that point, did you begin to be influenced by any other singers?

Joe: Well, I liked Tony Bennett, Percy Mayfield, Sammy Davis Jr., Nat King Cole, Billy Daniels, Sara Vaughn, and Carmen McRae.

Imp: So, how's N.Y. treating you?

Joe: I've appeared with many top groups and travelled along the Eastern sea coast, working with other groups. I would find I'd have to limit my repertoire to the music they know. At that point I began to organize my own group, consisting of five hand-picked musicians that relate to a positive mood in music and also in life.

Imp: Since that point, when you organized your group, what kind of changes have you experienced?

Joe: Well, I've become more aware of politics in relation to dealing with all phases of life...in choosing tunes, the places where you work. I also feel that the purpose of music is to lift the consciousness of the average person to a higher level.

Imp: Yes. Do you see yourself as a singer fulfilling a particular function?

Joe: Yes, I feel a part of the master plan...a piece of the puzzle. The master plan being controlled by the total universe, directed by cosmic powers.

Imp: How do you think the majority of Black people relate to your music?

Joe: Jazz is for a select few, never for the total. It will never die, for the select few will keep it alive through generations.

Imp: Do you see jazz as a spiritual force drawing people together?

Joe: Definitely I feel as Black people we must be totally educated politically, meaning we must create our own jobs, which means economic support and financial independence. For this reason, I created a studio for open rehearsals, and also, a place for musicians to gather and exchange ideas.

Imp: Where is this again?

Joe: It's the Ladies Fort and Alley Gallery at No. 2 Bond Street. There are matinees every Saturday and Sunday from 4-7 P.M. ✿

RON VAN CLIEF

Cont'd from page 57

what they're doing. Once you develop your basic form, you develop the essence of what you're doing, and if you just work on the form itself, you can develop your mind and your body. It's very disciplined, so through the discipline you develop freedom. In martial arts, freedom is equal to power. What happens is once you develop freedom of most of your restrictive ideas, you develop complete and total awareness of what's around you, then you can do anything. So it's not really difficult. It's a very simple art, karate. The most strenuous part is the method of making yourself go that one extra step, for that one extra mile. The drop-out rate in martial arts is high because they don't want discipline.

See, they want to train and not sweat or work out, or whatnot, and get to black belt level or whatever, but without that training. And back to the levels of the black belts, the third-degree black belt is called Sensei, which means teacher.

Imp: Are there certain truths that you've been initiated into that you can't really speak about?

V: What do you mean? Such as...?

Imp: Well the truths I haven't been exposed to myself, but I've been told that in Zen, for instance, there's an old proverb about a Zen teacher. When he was asked what is Zen, he just didn't say anything. He was completely silent.

V: I don't know about that. I think that Zen should be learnt and not taught.

Imp: Learnt and not taught? Do you create the aura...?

V: Yes. Well, I teach Zen psychotherapy separate from the class. And we discuss the origins of the universe. That's really what it is.

Imp: Yet, without the proper understanding of the application it would be like...

V: Just understanding that that is a truth in itself is something. Most people are not even aware of the existence of the origin and the total concept of what Man is into. That's not just martial arts. That covers the total life cycle of what you start with and what you end up with, and nothing can change that. ✿

ED BULLINS

Cont'd from page 42

the best, all things considered. (laughs)

Imp: Like what?

Bullins: All things considered. (laughs)

Imp: Oh.

Bullins: I mean, the amount of my work, the number of things I have that can hold an audience for the whole evening. I'm to theater what Muhammad Ali is to boxing. And I intend to hold my crown for a while. (laughs) ✿

Following is a partial list of the plays of Ed Bullins: *In the Wine Time; The Duplex; Clara's Ole Man; In New England Winter; Goin' a Buffalo; The Fabulous Miss Marie; The Taking of Miss Janie;* and *The Gentleman Caller.*

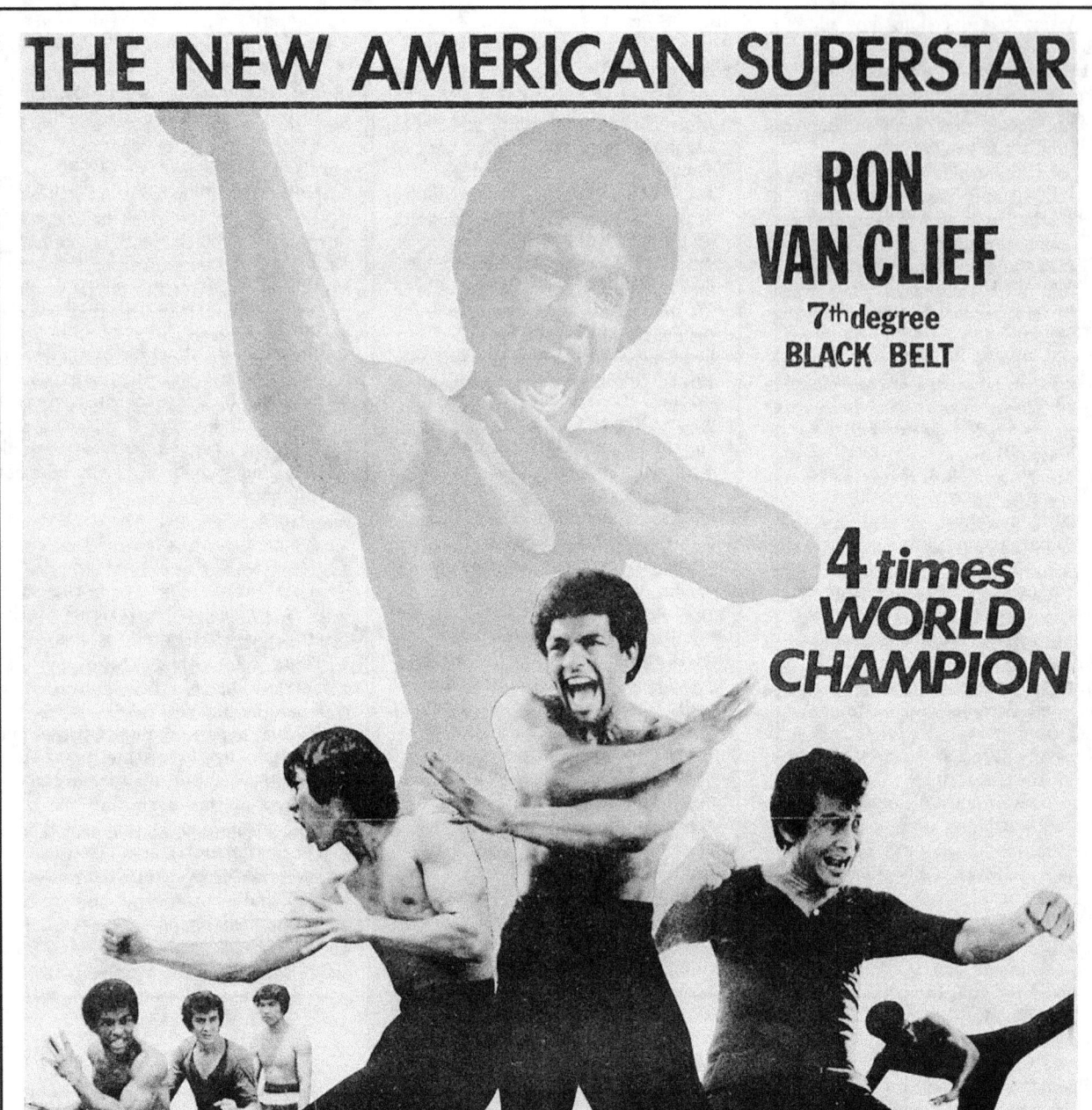

THE NEW AMERICAN SUPERSTAR

RON VAN CLIEF
7th degree
BLACK BELT

4 times
WORLD CHAMPION

Courtesy of Madison World Film

THE BLACK DRAGON

interview by Bob Bryan

Impressions: It's been said, Ron, that if one really wishes to be a master of an art, technical knowledge of it is not enough. One has to transcend techniques so that the art becomes an artless art, growing out of the subconcious. Do you go along with that?

Ron Van Clief: All martial arts are a combination of the mental, physical and spiritual, and therefore the development of the human being, of the individual. To acclimate to the environment, in order to sustain itself, become one with the environment, this is true harmony.

Imp: Are there particular techniques that one goes into to develop this?

V: There are various art forms that one can go into to develop this, some more so than others. Karate, that's a very primitive form of martial art because it deals primarily with basic physics, speed plus time plus focus equals power. But when you deal with a martial art like Aikijitsu, which is a form translated to mean "capabilities of source", this a low-energy input martial art; whereas karate is a high-energy input, structurally. Aikijitsu can be done by anyone. Karate is very strenuous. I wouldn't recommend karate for everybody.

Imp: Is that because of their physical makeup?

V: Their mental makeup and their physical makeup.

Imp: How so the mental?

V: Karate itself is an aggressive martial art. Kicking, punching...this type of conditioning builds aggressiveness which you let out when sparring. It's only through the Zen training -- through zeal, energy and nowness that you develop yourself and become aware of your potentialities. You don't need to ego trip or whatever. Most people who are into karate are what I consider paranoid of the environment. They need something to bolster their ego in order to really function. Martial arts serve as therapy. They condition the individual so that he can function. So that relaxation is not just a word; it means that you have to take time out to relax. Being relaxed and taking time out to relax are two different things. Relaxation should be natural.

Imp: With the unmoved center?

V: Yes. The Hara, the Kime, how you develop your basic breathing in order to find your center line.

Imp: Why is breathing important?

V: Proper breathing keeps you from becoming exhausted. More air going to the blood brings more iron, which brings more oxygen, which rejuvenates you. Your body is like a machine. With the proper diet and proper breathing and proper exercise, of course, it perpetuates your system. Most people don't breathe properly. They breathe from here (indicating lungs). You should breathe from the lower part of your diaphragm. The Japanese call this area the hara. This is where you constantly clean out your respiratory system. Short breaths don't even let the lungs work. So as soon as you become exhausted from any type of physical exertion you're truly exhausted because your breathing has not been synchronized with your movement.

Imp: And the diet?

V: Well, I'm a vegetarian. I haven't eaten meat for seven years.

Imp: How has it affected your performance?

V: Much better. I feel as though I'm working on natural energies more so than just carbohydrates and sugar. I find that my body runs more fluid. My stomach has not had the stomach problems it would have on an irregular diet. And meat takes too long to digest.

Imp: You have a Ph.D. in Zen psychotherapy. What exactly is Zen psychotherapy?

V: I have had ten years of Zen instruction. I was taught by my teacher, Master Peter, who is the founder of the National Academy of Martial Arts and Sciences. I've studied Zenshu, which is the martial arts religion, and Zen psychotherapy, which is the vehicle by which the Zen applies to the individual. For example, you take an axiom such as, "Defeat the self first to know." Now, in order to make this axiom work you have to understand yourself, which gives you introspective perception, which through having more perception, you develop an awareness of yourself that you really didn't have before. It's very objective, not subjective. Zen psychotherapy has many different guidelines, just as other forms of psychology. Zen, meaning zeal, energy and nowness, that means that once you become aware of yourself, you become positive through your PMA, "positive mental attitude," and you develop your whole self. See, martial arts, Zen psychotherapy is used to develop people, their personalities, their character, how to develop your entire self.

Imp: It's been said that teachers of Zen do not really teach Zen.

V: You can't really teach Zen. You're just making a person aware of something that they are and they're not aware of. A teacher opens up one's eyes to the view, the full view.

Imp: Do you prefer to deal with certain types of personalities in students as opposed to other types?

V: The challenge of Zen psychotherapy is total. It's a total martial arts concept wherein nothing is impossible. No matter how an individual might be as a student initially, via the conditioning processes, they change or they don't remain. But normally they come to the understanding that this change is good for them.

Imp: What if they use the art in the street?

V: I normally terminate them. There is no need for the physical confrontation in the street. I wouldn't let a person disturb my whole life for one second of their stupidity. You can put someone in the hospital, or kill them, for nothing, for zero. Now what sense does that make?

Imp: How do you feel that the martial arts films are affecting the community? It seems to cater to the aggressive element in people.

V: Well, that would be the original argument against all martial arts. People do not realize that it starts in a reaction against oppression and therefore take it to be corrupt. It started in India and went to China. From China it went to Okinawa where they developed the term "karate," meaning "empty-handed, hand in air." The development of the open-arm method, to what we know now. The Japanese invaded Okinawa, they forbade the carrying of weapons, so they had to use another form. The Japanese thought of this as a functionable, usable system. Then it spread all over the world.

Imp: Would you say that your educational background is unusual for a martial artist?

V: Yes and no. Once a martial artist becomes advanced, of course they seek higher realms. I also went to school for the martial arts.

Imp: Is it here in New York? Through what university?

V: Yes, it's here in New York. The University of Martial Arts and Sciences.

Imp: Can you talk about your new screenplay?

V: This film is the sequel to "The Black Dragon," which is the film that is out now. The original title of the new film was "The Legend of the Hungry Tiger." It's about two brothers who were brought up in Brooklyn and they go through a lot of things in the university of the streets and they both take martial arts. But one doesn't understand the full meaning of the martial arts.

He's under a heavy ego trip, and they split up because of this. The other one is going to college and he's doing this FBI thing and he becomes sort of like a CIA James Bond type agent. And the other brother gets involved in a drug operation, organized crime. And eventually they both meet and one has to kill the other one. It could be considered similar to the "French Connection," the bust on top of the bust, the counter-bust.

Imp: Is this the beginning of a series of films?

V: Well, I've written ten screenplays and I intend to start my own company. I've already begun to acquire equipment.

Imp: How will your martial arts films differ from others?

V: In the reality of the technique. Most of the techniques that we use in the martial arts films are very sloppy. They are not accurate, they are not precise, and they are not economical. So this is basically a blasphemy because it's not adhering to the basic curriculum of martial arts ideology.

Imp: Do you think these elements can be portrayed in a film and still make it commercially feasible to depict them?

V: You have to show not only the man's physical superiority, the hero, but you have to show the mental superiority. The calmness, the relaxed attitude, the ability to deal with extreme situations under duress, and with systematic logic.

Imp: What is systematic logic?

V: Systematic logic is being able to adapt to any situation, no matter how detrimental, with a clear, unclogged mind.

Imp: If someone were to attack you in the street for no reason, how would you react? For instance, if he came at you with a club?

V: A club is a very simple weapon to defend yourself against. You understand that any weapon is an extension of the active hand. Being able to understand this at a glance, the person's stance evaluation, where the weight is displaced, what hand the weapon is in, if the hand is farther from you or closer to you, which hand is closer, the primary or critical distance, and understanding the capabilities of the body. With the martial arts ideology you understand totally at a glance what that is. It's like a picture.

Imp: Does the technique come first, and instinct come second?

V: It's the same thing. Through repetition you develop a technique. What that does is develop your blocking systems, your side-stepping and body-shifting devices.

Imp: And your mind is transcended, too?

V: Of course. Fighting is not violent. It becomes strictly academic. Understanding the basic nature of a person in the street. If they had a club, they would definitely try to hit you in the face, try to knock out the computer. So, basically, a person who would strike at an area that is the smallest really isn't together, because it is much easier to block the head. So they attack the head and you spontaneously counter-attack and you take out first the lower areas...the knees, groin, what we call the motivational system, legs, etc. Then the abdomen, which is your respiratory and breathing apparatus and then the computer. So that's how you do it economically and scientifically.

Imp: Are there various points on the body which must be given specific consideration in terms of the execution of specific techniques?

V: No, because all the techniques that we learn can be applied to whatever manner or degree of power and force. It's not necessary to do structural bodily harm. Through the use of this form of Aikijitsu you develop entrapping exercises like chokes, levers and locks. If you put a person under high-intensity pain, say you put a good wrist lock on the arm, and grab the windpipe with your other hand, the person cannot breathe...intense pain, shock and no air. And you didn't have to break the person's arm and he didn't have to have a concussion.

Imp: Is it possible to reach a higher state in which it's not even necessary to physically deal with the person?

V: Yes, of course. When you reach that state, we call this having acquired Chi, which is the internal force. Your body is like an electrical circuit. It all depends upon the nature of the person and the type of mind that you have-where there is a positive there has to be a negative. Disregarding punching or kicking, this is all figured in your head. And through verbalizing, you are like mesmerizing an individual, there really is no need to.

Imp: Do you think that violent Black movies help to create an atmosphere for violence within the community?

V: I don't believe that. I believe that within the Black community they should have more martial arts and a planned martial arts program in all communities so that the people can develop, not just so that they understand kicking and punching. But the martial arts is only 20% physical and

80% mental. A lot of people have the wrong idea about martial arts.

Imp: Yet weapons are used in the martial arts.

V: Any weapon is just an extension of the empty hand.

Imp: In striking out at an object, do you achieve that point of focus immediately?

V: Yes, it's just as if you have your own sighting device mechanism. It's like having your own computer.

Imp: Where is your school located?

V: At 62 West 14th Street. The University of Martial Arts & Sciences.

Imp: Is it open to the community?

V: It's open from 6 to 9, Monday through Friday.

Imp: If someone wanted to enter a program of instruction in order to improve their physical and spiritual well-being, what steps would you recommend they take?

V: Find a good school. You've got to rate the school, you've got to rate the instructor.

Imp: How can you do that if you've had no experience?

V: You can tell by looking at the students. If the students are good, that means that the instructor is good. If the students have a poor attitude or a poor technique, then the instructor is not instructing them properly.

Imp: Could a person study at home before enrolling in a school?

V: Well, they have a lot of material that you can read. There are many books by Lao-Tsu.

Imp: How has Zen psychotherapy, as well as the martial arts, transformed your life?

V: It's made a complete difference in my life. Imagine the basic future that a person has, a Black person coming from the ghetto, and developing from Brooklyn to Broadway. It's important that the basic ideology of martial arts, things like positive mental attitude, or the "iron will," what this really can do. "Plan your work, work your plans." That's from Lao-Tsu. It's made me understand the full range of human potentiality.

Imp: Is it unlimited?

V: Unlimited, yes.

Imp: Is Man more than just Man on this planet?

V: Of course.

Imp: What is your idea of Man?

V: I think that the mind of Man is the most superior thing in the cosmic universe, because everything was created from the mind of Man. There are only two realities: living and dying. The rest are illusions that are believed.

Imp: Is one dying now...does one live later?

V: Physically you die now, but live later, spiritually.

Imp: Does that get into reincarnation?

V: Yes.

Imp: Is that just a projection, a fantasy?

V: I don't know that it is a fantasy.

Imp: Are you aware of living other lives in the past?

V: Yes and no. I find that I do believe in reincarnation because the shell that we have now may last for a hundred years or less, and I don't think that Man was created for such a short life span. The process of aging starts as soon as you're born, and you're depleting yourself as you go. So you have to develop yourself, complete your cycle by developing a healthy personality.

Imp: What do you mean by the use of the word "positive" in PMA..."positive mental attitude"?

V: Positive is relevant, doing what is economical, functional, for self-development. What is positive perpetuates your own existence. And by perpetuating your own existence you perpetuate everyone's existence because you're part of the universe. If you develop yourself, through martial arts ideology, you develop the people around you. Of course, it makes everything work much smoother. Also, it may be positive within that person's framework of reality. It doesn't necessarily mean that the act or whatever transpired was in essence true. So of course the reality changes with the individual. What is true in your framework of reality may not be true in my framework of reality.

Imp: So is there one ideology?

V: The one ideology is the Zen, the Zenshu, the martial arts religion. And this develops so that you can change. See, Lao-Tsu said, "Change is constant." In order to progress, or to evolve, you have to change, to acclimate to the environment or the changes in the environment. And that's what it is. That's what the whole thing comes down to.

Imp: Going through changes. Now in the street...

V: The world going through changes, and you maintaining the same changes so that you're at harmony with your environment. You can change and not be in harmony with...For example, a Black man with a white woman in South Carolina is not in harmony there. Here it may be, and yet many people may be against this. But of course it's accepted.

Imp: Must one prostitute his values when he feels that certain people have not reached this level of understanding?

V: No.

Imp: So who's in tune and who's out of tune?

V: You're in tune as long as whatever you're doing is still maintaining the original course that you set. For example, five years ago I was with the Negro Ensemble Company in the screenplay workshop there with Steve Carter. And he gave a lot to my head, upstairs, mechanically, for writing. I think the impression I got from Steve was that the development should be not just on a martial arts level, but on a mental level. He got my ideas together as far as acting, the methodology of acting. And acting is the same as doing martial arts. Of course, if you are at rest with yourself, whatever you do in going to coincide with the environment, anyway. Because you can't change your initial character. You can only change your attitude towards what you're doing once you understand who you are. And that's what Zen

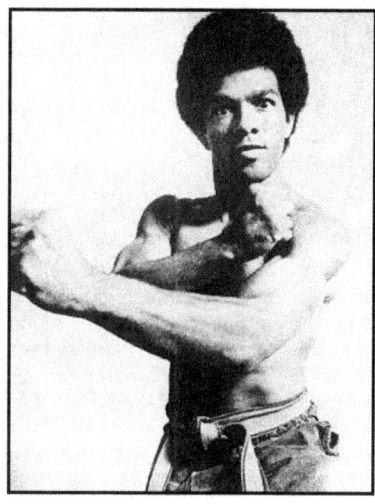

psychotherapy does for you. It makes you understand, without a doubt, who you are, where you're going, and where you came from.

Imp: How would you describe your own character?

V: I can only say that...I cannot evaluate my own character. You may be able to evaluate my character. I can give you what I think it is, but of course this may not be true. But most of the people that I grew up with, the young guys, 60% of them have died from either war-- I was in Vietnam, my brother died there also--drugs, alcohol, and no exercise, cardiac. So it has changed for me. It's given me a better image of who I am, and if you want to project the correct image, you have to stay in the proper mental, physical and spiritual shape.

Imp: Do you feel you have a

destiny?

V: Well, my objective in studying martial arts is to make the world understand that there are Black masters in martial arts, also. We've been under the misconception for so many years that the whites and the Orientals are superior martial artists, and in martial arts the individual adapts to the martial arts, not the martial art to the individual. So you cannot really say that an Oriental would be superior because they started before us. The Americans have meat, they are larger, they are structured bigger, and, basically, they like to fight.

Imp: Do you mean meat in a positive sense?

V: Yes, meat. The meat diet. Japanese, Chinese, all these people basically are small. So you can't say that the guy weighing 130 pounds, no matter what rank he is, is going to beat a guy weighing 195 pounds. And if the person has any technique at all, I think definitely the large person would win, for real, under real circumstances. But in school or practicing, of course, the guy that's quicker will win.

Imp: You're a seventh degree black belt. What does that mean?

V: We'll start with the basic rank structure. White belt — initial stage. Green belt — intermediate. Purple belt, brown belt, then black belt. The first level of black belt is called the Shodan Ho. This means probationary black belt. You're working to attain your full first degree. At that point you're not allowed to teach. You're just a student at that point. Then you have your second degree black belt which is your senior expert. And your third degree black belt which is your teaching level. Your fourth and fifth are your lower master levels. Your sixth and seventh start the Kyoshi level, which means "risen" or "better." At this stage you apply for your Ph.D. in martial arts.

Imp: Is it just a matter of technique?

V: Yes technique, Kata, free fighting, breaking techniques, etc. In order to become a teacher, you have to be a champion, first of all, and you have to be a teacher. Most people that take martial arts are not made out to be teachers.

Imp: What are the characteristics of a teacher?

V: To teach martial arts you should have at least six years in martial arts, so you not only understand the basic physical mechanics but the mental mechanics of what you're doing. A lot of people are in martial arts for ten years and they never understand the true mechanics of

Cont'd on page 53

THE REVOLUTIONARY GROWTH OF AN ENSEMBLE

by Bob Wisdom

As recently as 1971, if anyone can believe, the jazz community in New York approached its second coming. Young musicians emulated the greats from earlier periods; established musicians experimented with new fusions — with a predominance of rock; and the clear-cut innovators were in Europe being appreciated. Artists were hit with a sort of future shock. Social phenomenons guided the direction of the music. Jazz became the healing force of the universe. Spirituality layered much of the sounds, and with some groups this bordered on outright gimmickry. The casual observer knew not of what was going on, but just as in the apposite parallel cases of the Oedipus Complex and Original Sin, we suffered less before we knew what the disease was called. This affliction is not our own but brought on by the music industry. It's called "under-exposure" and is remedied by hearing one of the most emotionally powerful groups in this post-Coltrane era — THE REVOLUTIONARY ENSEMBLE. (After listening to them it's hard to settle for pap.)

This transitory phase affected, to some extent, the range and sound of most groups, but this talented string-percussive trio towers above the run of the mill horn-bass-drum-piano groups of which there are many.

This phase also ingrained the alignment of the music industry. Producers have suggested to the Ensemble that they change from upright to electric bass, add a keyboard and guitar, and the drummer change to rock licks in order to get "THE SOUND." None of these producers can see beyond the top ten of Billboard, for the revolutionary Ensemble is truly one the most original groups of our times.

For violinist Leroy Jenkins, Chicagoan fresh from a tour in Europe with the Creative Construction Company (their members were Anthony Braxton, Leo Smith, Muhal Richard Abrams, Richard Davis and Steve McCall), any illusion he had of New York didn't last long. After playing twenty-five-dollar gigs around New York, and enduring for years the short-sightedness of the Be-Bop groups, whose concepts didn't allow for a violin, Jenkins became more determined to become part of a group. Profoundly affected by his experience with the Association for Advancement of Creative Musicians (AACM), their concept of collectives rather than leader-sideman, and the musical direction that emanate from this mid-western center, Leroy wanted something along these lines.

Similar frustrations were felt by Atlanta-born bassist Sirone. In New York since the mid-Sixties, Sirone has recorded with a host of artists — among them, Marion Brown and Pharaoh Sanders. But through it all, he never felt he was able to develop as he felt he should. This was a justifiable feeling, because, through the Ensemble, Sirone has emerged as one of the most forceful and imaginative bassists on the scene. But during this period, this totally committed musician, whose daunting skill has flung him to the forefront of the jazz scene, fulfilled the solely supportive capacity of timekeeper.

Sirone, Leroy and drummer Frank Clayton joined in 1970 and formed the REVOLUTIONARY ENSEMBLE. With the New Music community as financially anemic as it is, and the group's rehearsal times as long as they are, Clayton was unable to stay with the group. After opting for a steadier source of income, Clayton's seat was filled by Chicagoan-come-New Yorker Jerome Copper, and the style and experience of the young but brilliant drummer filled out the trio as we know it.

Over seventy-five years of musical experience is represented in the Ensemble. Jenkins and Be-Bop, Sirone through the 50's and 60's, and Copper from the new Chicago scene, Europe and Africa. This explains the range of their music from contemplative to highly energized. The bluesy undertone of their material comes from both Chicago and Atlanta backgrounds, while the Afro-European rhythms are with Jerome Copper.

The Ensemble does not merely play their music; they explode. It won't be played in disco's, elevators, or shopping centers, and probably won't be heard on popular jazz stations, primarily because these are audiences used to passive music. The directness and color of the music has grown largely unmitigated since the group's inception. Each musician does his part in contributing to the mood of the music, from Leroy playing fast, repeated figures on the viola over ostinato riffs by the unit, to Sirone on bow, playing such astounding aico duets with Leroy that it would make many of their classical contemporaries return to class. The threesome's ideas are combined in a suite; a motif is derived and improvisation takes place within this framework. I've left sets with the Ensemble feeling like I've just come from an invigorating therapeutic massage. You find yourself sitting up straight in your seat, back muscles rippling. As Leroy contends, "...we play with no frills and no pretensions, but there definitely is a structure, a motif, and ours is without time, basis or chords, but a structure is still present..."

REVOLUTIONARY ENSEMBLE has minimized the distracting elements of the music world by incorporating themselves into the RE: Records. They have eliminated the influence of the less-that-gifted producers. They in turn have delegated various business chores amongst themselves. The group's business is their own.

The Ensemble has produced three critically-acclaimed albums of their own: VIETNEM I & II, on ESP Disk; MANHATTAN CYCLES on India Navigation, and the latest entitled "THE PSYCHE," on their own RE Records.

Despite a growing demand for the group on college campuses and around the world, the unit is largely inactive during the summer. This is not threatenin to the members, because they are totally committed to their music and understand fully the complexities of their world. Although they don't knock their contemporaries who have gone the more lucrative route, and have themselves been told to change their sound and name to gain acceptance, they are determined to make it on their own terms. They are determined to turn the listening habits of Americans away from the 19th-century harmonies and passivity to music that speaks of now and reflects the turmoil and experiences we are living.

When and if they move with a major label, they will take with them an audience which recognizes their credibility. They will also have a more than myopic viewpoint on the industry, and a full understanding of the games involved. Let's hope that history doesn't prove correct in this case and the group is "discovered" five or ten years from now. But meanwhile, the unit sees its own schema, and with the same fevor, intensity, seriousness and perserverance that is embodied in their music, they will rechart the path of music. For once "REVOLUTIONARY" is used to describe something other than insipid and vapid creations within traditional structures, somethingthat truly challenges the aesthetic framework of any culture. This unit will etch for themselves a place as one of the most remarkable and original units to emerge in the Seventies. ✿

record releases

LONDON

Olympic Runners	Out in Front	PS 658
Al Green	Al Green Explores Your Mind	SHL 32087

TICO

Eddie Palmieri	Eddie Palmieri Recorded Live at Sing Sing	CLP 1321
Tito Puente & His Orch.	Tito Unlimited	CLP 1322
Ismael Rivera	Traigo De Todo	CLP 1319
La Lupe	Un Encuentro Con La Lupe	CLP 1323

ALEGRE

Cabrerita Y sus Ideas	Explorando El Ambiente	CPLA 7010
Charlie Palmieri Y Su Orch.	Vuelve El Gigante	CLPA 7008

FOLKWAYS

Black Drama w/Barbara Ann Teer and Charlie Russell		FL 9712
The Montgomery Express	The Montgomery Movement	STS 33868
Juanita Johnson & The Gospel Tones	Climbing High Mountains	FTS 31037
East New York Ensemble of Music	At the Helm	FTS 33867
Sterling A. Brown	16 Poems of Sterling A. Brown	FL 9794
Arbee Stidham	There's Always Tomorrow	FTS 31033
Edgar Kendricks	Getting it Together	FC 7555
Bob Kirkpatrick	Feeling the Blues	FTS 31032
Sarah Webster Fabio	Soul Ain't Soul Is	FL 9711
Memphis Slim	Favorite Blues Singers	FA 2387

MERCURY

Eric Mercury		SRM 1-1026

RE: RECORDS

Revolutionary Ensemble	The Psyche	RE 3117

20TH CENTURY

Etta Jones		W-203
Leon Haywood	Come and Get Yourself Some	T-476
Melvin Sparks		W-204
Funkadelic	Let's Take It to the Stage	W-215
Fantastic Four	Alvin Stone: The Birth and Death of a Gangster	W-201
Smoked Sugar		T-473

ARISTA

Andrew Hill	Spiral	AI 1007
Tamiko Jones	Love Trip	AL 4040
Dewey Redman	Look for the Black Star	AL 1011
Paul Bley	Copenhagen and Haarlem	AL 1901
Stanley Cowell	Brilliant Circles	AL 1009
Jon Hendricks	Tell me the Truth	AL 4043
Larry Young's Fuel		AL 4051
Anthony Braxton	New York, Fall 1974	AL 4032
Roland Hanna	Perugia (Live at Montreux '74)	AL 1010
The Brecker Bros.		AL 4037
The Eleventh House Featuring Larry Corryell	Level One	AL 4052
Gil Scott-Heron and Brian Jackson	The First Minute of a New Day	A 4030
Oliver Lake	Heavy Spirits	AL 1008
Linda Lewis	Not a Little Girl Anymore	AL 4047

ATLANTIC

Stanley Clarke		NE 431
Billy Cobham	Total Eclipse	SD 18121
Duke Ellington	Recollections of the Big Band Era	SD 1665

BIOGRAPH

Scott Joplin	Scott Joplin-1916	BLP-1006Q
Johnny Shines & Co.		BLP-12048
Dan Smith	God is Not Dead	BLP-12036
Big Daddy/Bukka White		BLP-12049

AVCO

The Chambers Bros.	Right Move	AV-69003-698 8
The Stylistics	Thank you Baby	AV-69008-698 8

ABC/BLUE THUMB

The Crusaders	Chain Reaction	BTSD-6022

ABC

Sylvia Smith	Woman of the World	ABCD-876
Bobby Bland	Get on Down with Bobby Bland	ABCD-895
Rufus Featuring Chaka Khan	Rufusized	ABCD-837
The 5th Dimension	Earthbound	ABCD-897

EUBIE BLAKE MUSIC

Eubie Blake	Live Concert	EBM-5
Eubie Blake Introducing Jim Hession		EBM-6

WARNER BROS.

Jimmy Cliff	Music Maker	MS 2188

ISLAND RECORDS

Bob Marley & the Wailers	Natty Dread	ILPS 9281
Bob Marley & the Wailers	Catch a Fire	SW 9329
Bob Marley & the Wailers	Burnin'	ILPS 9256

PUBLISHER ACKNOWLEDGEMENTS

The rebirth of the Special 1974 Commemorative Reissue Series of IMPRESSIONS Magazine of the Arts
is a special labor of Love for us. 1974 witnessed an explosion of powerful & creative expressions in:
Theater Arts, Poetry, Art, Music, Photography, Literature, Dance / Choreography,
Theater Review, Film, Critique, Nutritional Advice & Fashion.

As the independent Publisher of IMPRESSIONS MAGAZINE OF THE ARTS I am very proud to be able to again
re-introduce to this new generation, the power and fertile imagination of these generous and talented contributing
artists and creators, who worked so hard to honestly represent themselves and their people
during this tumultuous, passionate and exciting period.
IMPRESSIONS MAGAZINE is truly a historical and educational snapshot of the times.

BOB MARLEY	CALVIN WILSON
MAYA ANGELOU	HERB HENRY
JAMES BALDWIN	HECTOR LINO, JR.
ED BULLINS	BRENDA BAILEY
D'URVILLE MARTIN	NIKKI COLEMAN
RON VAN CLIEF	BOB WISDOM
JOHN OLIVER KILLENS	MICHAEL HYATT
NOVELLA NELSON	YVONNE MORAN
JOE LEE WILSON	ROBERT BRYAN
MARTIE CHARLES	VIOLA BURLEY
C.O. SIMPKINS, M.D.	COLLEEN CANNON
EARL 'FATHA' HINES	ED LEAK
MEL WRIGHT	BOB ELLISON
LESLIE JEAN-BART	MARTHA SWOPE

GV SERIES IMPRESSIONS Magazine of the Arts Publications

GV16 **IMPRESSIONS Magazine of the Arts (December 1974)** -Reissue Date 07/29/2012
GV17 **IMPRESSIONS Magazine of the Arts (Spring 1975)** - Reissue Date 08/15/2012
GV18 **IMPRESSIONS Magazine of the Arts (October 1975)** - Reissue Date 08/19/2012
GV19 **IMPRESSIONS Magazine of the Arts (June 1976)** - Reissue Date 12/2012

With much love & respect, I sincerely thank you from the top of my heart.

Robert Bob Bryan, Founder / Publisher
Loida Bryan, Co-Executive Producer
website: http://www.graffitiverite.com
e-mail: bryworld@aol.com

www.ingramcontent.com/pod-product-compliance
Lightning Source LLC
Chambersburg PA
CBHW081242180526
45171CB00005B/515